Copyright © 2018 by Steve Zanella

Cover and interior design by Steve Zanella

All rights reserved. This book or any portion thereof may not be reproduced or used in any manner whatsoever without the express written permission of the publisher except for the use of brief quotations in a book review.

The author of this book is not a licensed therapist or medical doctor. He does not dispense medical advice or prescribe the use of any techniques as a form of treatment for physical, emotional, or medical problems without the advice of a physician, either directly or indirectly. The intent of the author is to use his personal experiences with anxiety and panic disorder as a general guide to assist the reader with their emotional and spiritual well-being, but not as a replacement to current treatments or medications.

First Printing, 2018

ISBN: 978-1-7327797-1-6

www.stevezanella.com

The Anxiety Dharma

ONE MAN'S GUIDE FOR LIVING AN ANXIETY-FREE LIFE.

STEVE ZANELLA

For Deanna, Lilianne, Noah, and Camden.

TABLE OF CONTENTS

Introduction i

Chapter 1: The Power of Choice 1

Chapter 2: Finding Your Why 13

Chapter 3: Change Your Story 27

Chapter 4: Understanding Your Thoughts 37

Chapter 5: Living Mindfully – Becoming Present 51

Chapter 6: Positive Self-Talk 69

Chapter 7: Give to Receive 93

Chapter 8: Discovering the Core of Your Anxiety 109

Chapter 9: Practice with Intention 125

Chapter 10: Fear vs. Danger 147

Chapter 11: How to Forgive 165

Chapter 12: Focusing Your Mind 183

Epilogue: Bringing it All Together 203

Acknowledgments 211

About the Author 212

"Nothing can harm you as much as your own thoughts unguarded."
– Buddha

INTRODUCTION

I always wanted to be a father. As far back as I could remember, I wanted to have children. So, you would naturally assume that in June 2006, when my daughter, Lilianne, was born, it would have been the happiest moment of my life. And in many ways, it was.

My entire life up had been building to this. Up until that point, I had successfully checked off many of the to-do items from my "happy life" checklist:

Get a job: Check.
Get married: Check.
Buy a home: Check.
Have a child: Check.

This was all supposed to make me happy, right? It was all meant to fill in the gaps and finish the perfect picture that was my life. It was everything I ever wanted and had been working toward. But, in the excitement and joy of that moment, something felt wrong. Something felt incomplete.

They say everything changes when you have a child. That was certainly true for me. I guess how much things change greatly depends on where you are in life at the time. I thought I knew a lot about who I was before my daughter was born. I thought I had a pretty decent handle on the direction my life was heading. But what I didn't realize was that it was all about to change.

I love the analogy of a sweater with a loose thread. That once you begin to pull on that thread, the entire sweater begins to unravel.

This was my life: a sweater with a loose thread. That loose thread always seemed to be there. Every major life choice I made, that thread was there, sticking out, begging to be pulled. In the days and months after my daughter was born, I felt that thread gain. It was the feeling that something was wrong. I always knew that thread existed. But either consciously or subconsciously, I never dared pull it.

It is often said that we make all life decisions from either a place of love or fear. I thought the reason I never pulled that thread was out of love. The love I felt for the people in my life: my wife, my parents, my brothers and sister, my friends. I never wanted them to feel hurt, suffer, or feel sadness or pain. But in truth, I never pulled that thread because of fear.

I was afraid of what I might find when that thread began to unravel. That sweater was my protection, not theirs. It shielded me from the outside world. I built it. I created it. I needed to keep it intact because it shielded me from everything I told myself I was shielding others from. Pain. Sadness. Hurt.

It represented every choice I ever made and every belief I ever had. If I didn't have that sweater, who would I be? I would be naked. I would be left out, exposed to the world. Others might see that my choices were not correct or that my beliefs couldn't hold up to their scrutiny. The idea of being judged was a fate far worse than death to me. I had spent years crafting the story that now had become my life. It was careful. It was meticulous. It was safe. If I didn't have that, what did I have? Who would I be?

The thing about love and fear is that they are both very powerful. And whichever one has the strongest hold over your heart makes the majority of decisions. My entire life had been built with a fearful heart. I hadn't taken any risks. I had always taken the safe path whenever it was presented.

That didn't mean I always chose the path with the greatest chance for success. It meant I chose the path that represented the least amount of discomfort. I was afraid of hurting and feeling uncomfortable. But it's surprising how comfortable you can become with things that don't make you feel happy or inspired. Growth requires risk and feeling uncomfortable. When you avoid those things, you stifle your ability to learn, expand, and love. You stifle the very things that make life worth living.

When that fear takes over your life, it has a name. It's called anxiety. I suffered from anxiety my entire life. From my years as a child, through my teenage years and into my adult life, anxiety had always been there. I just didn't know it had a name, or that it was a disorder. I didn't know how powerful it could be.

In my mind, this feeling was just… life. I thought this was how my mind worked, how my life was. My days were narrated by a negative, worried stream of thoughts, critiquing my every action and desire. Each moment was analyzed, each dream minimized. I thought there was something wrong with me. That somehow in the great lottery of life, I had been given a losing ticket. I had been cursed with a mind that looked at life not like an adventure to be enjoyed but as a suffrage to be endured.

My mind told me I was weak, flawed, worthless, stupid, talentless, lazy, and unworthy of truly being happy. It was as if my suffering was a sort of penance, that I had to live with in order to eventually earn happiness. That once I obtained a collection of the right things in life, this cloud would lift and I would feel happiness. But deep inside, I didn't believe that. I had decided this was the way life felt: a dull ache in the pit of my stomach, as if something bad was about to happen and there was nothing I could do to avoid it.

This is how anxiety makes you feel.

As I held my daughter in my arms, something shifted in me. That shift, I now understand, was the shift from fear to love. For the first time, the feeling of love had a stronger hold over my heart than fear. Looking down at this little, perfect person who had no choice but to love and trust me completely, I became filled by the power of this love. It was a feeling I hadn't felt in such a long time, not since I was small child. To me, love had always been tethered to pain. For every love you gained you owed something in return. But this love was not like that. This love was pure and easy. It flowed naturally and effortlessly.

She could do no wrong in my eyes. There was nothing my child could do or say, no choice she could make in life that would cause me not to love her with all my heart. In that moment of understanding, my mind became flooded with questions. Was I ever this perfect? Did my parents look at me like I looked at her? What had I done to make me no longer feel worthy of receiving this kind of love? Had I done anything at all?

Then fear crept in. What if she becomes anxious like me? What if she someday feels unworthy of love like I have? What would I tell her? How would I help her conquer the fear, negativity, and suffering that I had never been able to overcome?

This powerful stream of questioning aligned with the feeling of love, compelling me to do something I never wanted to do before. Something I had to do now, not for myself, but for her. I had no choice.

It was time to pull the thread.

I needed to understand how I had gone from being a perfect little child who could do no wrong, to a person who felt completely unworthy of receiving the unconditional love I was feeling for my daughter.

This book is a collection of everything that transpired before, during, and after I made that shift from fear to love. My hope is that sharing my experiences will serve as a guide for you to make your own shift, not because I tell you something but because you learn to see it within yourself. I've learned so much over the years thanks to my anxiety. They say, "When the student is ready, the teacher will appear." Once I learned to look at my life through a different lens, my anxiety became my greatest teacher.

That is why I decided to name this book The Anxiety Dharma, because the lessons I have learned from struggling to overcome my fear and anxiety are lessons that anyone can learn. If you suffer from anxiety, you have a great teacher inside you. Your anxiety can become a great source of inspiration, motivation, and understanding, opening you up to a new world of possibilities. A world that, until this point, has probably felt outside of your grasp. I'm here to tell you, you can grasp it!

What this book is not is a way to learn to hack your anxiety. It's not about quick fixes, shortcuts or easy tricks to make it go away.

I've tried many of those tricks. I've even had some level of success using the techniques taught in those types of books. But any positive experiences I've had only lasted for a short period of time. That was because anxiety is only a symptom of a deeper issue needing to be addressed. Like a headache or sore throat, anxiety points to a measurement of "dis-ease" that needs to be discovered and treated.

Unless you do the work to uncover the cause of your anxiety, any short-term success will eventually give way to new patterns or a re-occurrence of old symptoms. You need to address the root cause.

The tips and tools in this book are taught in conjunction with learning to change the views you've been taught and how you've been programmed to see your world. This is the most critical and difficult part of overcoming your anxiety.

In order to wake up to the idea that you can change your anxiety and fear into love, you must first allow yourself to be open to seeing how your life, worldviews, and perspective all work to keep you trapped in this way of thinking.

Your ego and your social conditioning will try and convince you that the world is the way it is and that your fear is based in reality and truth. That you should fear the world because it's a dark and dangerous place filled with bad people looking to do you harm. I'm here to tell you that, while this statement isn't false, it is only partially true. The world is filled with just as much light, with good people looking to help. How you focus your perspective is what causes you to see only one or the other.

Our thoughts and fears work to trick us into believing one over the other. My hope is that this book will open your heart and your mind to the idea that both are possible, and it's my personal experience that we are far more in control of these outcomes than we even know.

We are the creators of our world. We can choose to either create from a place of love or a place of fear. I want to help you learn to create from a place of love. But you must first learn how. And your anxiety is trying to teach you exactly that.

I welcome you to begin this journey with me. I promise that once you read this book and adopt just one of its teachings to your everyday practice, you will experience a change in your life. A change that will shift you from fear to love.

"We are our choices."
– Jean-Paul Sartre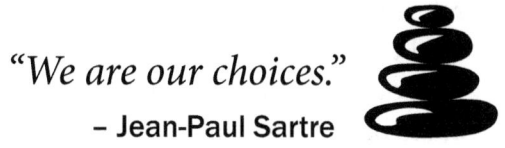

CHAPTER 1: THE POWER OF CHOICE

I was standing in the kitchen of our house, listening. I don't recall what was being said, I just remember listening. I was about three years old, and that kitchen seemed so large to me. The entire house seemed like a castle with massive rooms and all the space I needed. In truth, it was an average-sized house for our neighborhood in Natick, Massachusetts. It's funny how everything seems so much bigger when you're a child. If I walked into that house today, I'd probably wonder how a family fit into such a small house. But back then, it seemed enormous.

I was listening to something I would hear a lot over the course of my childhood: the raised voices of my parents.

They were arguing about something. The subject matter of the argument never seemed to interest me. I just remember their loud, angry voices and the sound of two people I loved very much not loving each other.

My mother was inside the house, but my father was not. He was standing on the stairs outside the front door that led into the kitchen. My mother had locked him out of the house and was refusing to let him back in.

I don't recall how long the two of them stood there yelling at each other through that door or how long I stood there listening. It could have been minutes or hours. Much like the size of our house, time seems flexible when you are a child. What I do remember is that, at one point, my father called out to me.

"Steven, it's your dad. Open the door and let me in the house."

My mother quickly turned and responded, "Steven, don't you open that door!"

I just stood there. I didn't know what to do. I had no idea how to process what was happening. Here were the two most important people in my life. Both of them were upset, and both were telling me to do the opposite thing. Do I listen to my dad and open the door? Do I listen to my mom and not open the door? What if I obey my mom and my dad gets mad at me? What if I obey my dad and my mom gets mad? Would my dad still love me if I didn't open the door? Would my mom still love me if I did? What do I do?

So I did the only thing I could do. I froze. I felt lost and alone. I was too scared to do anything, so I did nothing. I remember feeling conflicted over my options. Neither was a good one. I was being forced to decide between my mother and my father. Three years old was far too young an age to feel that type of pressure.

This was the first time I remember feeling what I now recognize as anxiety. I felt scared having to make a choice and what the outcome of that choice might be. There was no good choice in this situation. All choices were bad. And this would be a feeling that would echo throughout most of my life.

It's funny how a small moment in time can leave such an indelible mark on a person. I don't have many memories from my childhood. But I remember that moment, standing in that kitchen all those years ago. I didn't know it at the time, but this moment would set me down a path that would alter every action I would take, thought I would think, and emotion I would feel.

One of the greatest gifts we are given is our ability to choose. It is the moment everything begins to take shape: when we decide what we will do and say, the direction we'll take, and how we'll move forward.

When choice is seen as a bad thing or something to avoid, it stifles us mentally, emotionally, and even physically. When we are unable or unwilling to make a choice, or to fully understand why we make the choices we make, we are left feeling powerless, afraid, alone, and disheartened. We can't take action if we can't make choices. If we can't make good choices, we can't take good, well-thought-out steps toward creating a life we truly want or that will bring us happiness, fulfillment, joy, and abundance.

Each moment we live, we have the opportunity to make choices: what to eat, what to wear, where to live, with whom to interact, which job to pursue, and so on. Many of these choices we make without fully understanding why we make them. Even worse, and in my particular case, we don't make any choices at all. This, of course, is still a choice, but it's one that allows others to make choices for you, causing you to live a life decided by the pressure placed on you by others.

Eventually, we are all forced to make choices. When we are hungry, we must choose to eat or we starve. If we choose healthy food, we can take care of our bodies and our health. If we choose unhealthy foods, our bodies will suffer over time. Often, the desire for instant gratification causes us to choose things that may seem to make us happy in the short term but actually do us more harm than good down the road.

Even worse, many of us have no idea why we make the choices we make. We seem to be driven by an unseen hand, causing us to do things we don't understand and for reasons we aren't sure of.

Have you ever been hungry, gone to the refrigerator and looked inside for something to eat, only to find nothing of interest? You close the door and walk away, only to return moments later and look again as if something new may have magically appeared.

The choice to return and look again doesn't make rational sense. Often, we repeat this action of looking again and again, unaware we're even doing it. It's almost as if we're on autopilot, taking actions involuntarily without our control.

We do this not because we are hungry, but because we are bored. Whatever we are doing at that moment isn't enough to capture our full attention, so we look for something else that will give us a sense of fulfillment. For many, it's a sweet or salty snack. The action of looking and then looking again in the same place, over and over, is a choice we make but not one we seem to be aware we're making. We do it out of habit.

There are many factors that contribute to why we do things like this. The process of doing the same things over and over without fully being aware we are doing them repeats in many aspects of our lives. How many times have you end a romantic relationship with one person only to start dating almost the exact same type of person again. Or commit to yourself that you are going to get into better shape or make healthier food choices only to choose the couch or the cake over the gym or the salad? We tend to make the same mistakes over and over, never recognizing we are doing it until it is too late. Most of the motivation for such repetitive actions are buried very deep in the subconscious mind and may relate to something you experienced weeks, months, or years ago. The memory is still there, acting itself out through your actions, but you're unaware of its driving force.

I never understood why I panicked each time a choice was presented to me. Or why I seemed so willing to allow others to make major life decisions for me. When I did make a choice, it was often based on how I thought others would react or benefit from my choice. It was never based on what I wanted out of life. My choices were not my own, so my life always felt chaotic and out of my control.

And why wouldn't it? I was living a life everyone else thought I should be living. It was a life I had been programmed to believe I wanted but didn't actually want. Each choice life presented me with took me down a path that made me feel less comfortable and sure of myself – more uneasy, upset and anxious.

But the truth was, the secret to fixing it was always there, in front of me the entire time. *I had to learn to make better choices.*

This may sound obvious, but often the things right in front of us are the hardest to see because we are too close to it. It's like the saying goes: "You can't see the forest for the trees." I couldn't see I had a problem with choices because I didn't think I did. I was completely unaware of my issue with making choices or why I had this problem.

And honestly, it wasn't until years later, when I sat down and reflected over my life in preparation for a TEDx talk, that it even occurred to me where my problem with choice actually stemmed from.

That moment years ago, standing in my parents' kitchen, listening to them fight and asking me to choose which one of them I would obey. That moment set in motion a life of indecision, worry, stress, and anxiety that has taken me a lifetime to understand.

Don't take this the wrong way: I don't blame my issues or problems on the actions of my parents. They didn't set out to cause this anxiety in me. They didn't plan out the events that caused my fear of choice. They were just two people trying to figure out their own issues. Both of them had shortcomings to deal with that impacted the choices and actions of their lives. I just happened to get caught in the middle of that one moment, causing a ripple effect that would grow in size and importance through years of repetition and re-enforcement.

There was no malice in their action toward me, their child. But their lack of intent didn't lessen the impact of that moment for me. And until I was able to see my life through their perspectives, I would not fully be able to heal the psychological wounds from that moment – and the subsequent moments after.

But none of that would have been possible if I hadn't done one thing first. I had to make the choice to change my life. I had to do what to me, at the time, was unthinkable. I had to choose to take a different action, pick a different path, and take back my life.

It was the hardest thing I've ever done, but it was also the best decision.

And I say this now, in the first chapter of this book, for a reason. Because before you go any farther reading this book, you need to ask yourself if you are willing to make that same choice.

There is a reason you are where you are in your life. Many of you will point to the actions of others, situations that are outside of your control, or just that life hasn't been fair. And I'm here to tell you that is bullshit.

Your life is exactly the way it is because of the choices you've made. You may not be aware of why you've made these decisions, but they are still your choices. You are still responsible for making them, and you are currently living a life that represents the culmination of those choices.

The good news is that you also have the ability to make new decisions – today. Each moment we live, we have the ability to start over. We have the chance to choose to live our lives a new way, and we can make new choices that will have a positive impact on ourselves and those around us.

These choices aren't always easy and don't necessarily feel good when we make them. Especially if you are living a life built on poor choices. But, most likely, the life you are living already isn't easy and doesn't feel good. You are living that every day, choosing to hang on to things that no longer serve you because you are afraid that the pain you feel if you let go will be worse than the pain you feel already.

I'm here to ask you, what if by letting go of the things that no longer serve you, life doesn't get worse? What if your life gets much better?

Maybe your mind is telling you something like:

"But what if it doesn't get better?"

"There are no guarantees I won't make my life even worse!"

"He doesn't know my situation!"

"Easy for him to say, he's already done it and it worked out for him. What if I'm different?"

All of these are rational points, and you should allow yourself to have those thoughts. They are exactly the same thoughts I've had many times in my life, even when I made the choice to change my life. And that is the point you are at now.

Right now, you need to make a choice. You need to decide if you are going to use what you read in this book and take action: If you will apply the tools, approaches, and strategies outlined in the following chapters, or if you'll just read this book and move on to the next book, hoping it holds the secret to changing your life.

Let me save you the trouble. The secret to change your life is this: You must choose to be willing to take the actions that lead you to the life you want, figure out what those actions are, and then you must **physically take that action.**

Many of us search through countless books, videos, inspirational talks, online courses, and religious teachings for the secret to changing our lives. I know I did. I purchased every book I could get my hands on. I didn't actually practice or even fully read what was contained in those books, but I bought them. And after I bought them, I always felt a little better about myself. I always felt I was finally on the right path to fixing my life. My mind told me I was doing the right thing by buying this book, and that temporary feeling of joy was enough to make me feel good. This feeling lasted right up until I started reading the book.

At that point, it all seemed like work. Memorizing things, digging up my past, thinking about how to change things. Who had time for all that? My life was a mess *right now*. I needed to fix it *right now*. I don't have time to read an entire book. Just tell me what to do in the first chapter!

So here I am, writing my own book, and this is the first chapter. So for my younger self that might be reading this book now, let me tell you the biggest step you need to take that will guarantee either success or failure.

Ready?

You need to make the choice and take action. Nothing in this book, or any other book, will help you if you don't add these actions to your daily life. You need to develop the skills that will help you build the life you want rather than just settling for the life that is happening.

What most people don't consciously realize is that everything you do is a skill you had to practice. *Everything!* Breathing, walking, talking, eating, speaking, clapping, waving, playing an instrument, driving a car, using a computer, and anything else you now know how to do, you once didn't know how to do it and had to learn. You had to take action and develop the skill in order to go from not knowing how to knowing how.

This is the same with everything in life. Want to learn to paint? You have to practice putting paint onto a canvas with a brush. Want to learn how to build a house? You have to learn how to swing a hammer, use a saw, which materials to use, and how to connect them all in the proper order.

And if you want to learn how to build a better life, you need to learn what tools work for you. Then you need to practice using those tools over and over until they become second nature to you. Eventually, with enough practice, you will do these things without having to think about doing them, the same way you do things like eating or walking today.

It's something I like to call *practicing with intention*.

Every action you take, no matter how small, is the act of practicing toward learning a new skill. Every bad habit you currently have, every anxious thought, worrisome pattern, or destructive response to a situation is a result from the actions you have been practicing. Many of us have been practicing actions that have contributed to our anxiety and worry for so long, we are no longer aware of what those actions are. Our anxiety has become second nature, and the actions that support this behavior have entered into our subconscious behavior, invisible to our conscious mind.

This means we are doing things every day that continue to cause our anxiety to grow but we have become blind to what those actions are. And, while it is important to learn what those actions are so we can avoid repeating them, it is more important to work on practicing new daily actions so we may build healthier, more positive, and supportive habits.

I always tell people I had become a master at anxiety because I spent so many years practicing how to be anxious. I had mastered the skills of overthinking, negative self-talk, obsessive worry, and avoidance of suffering.

In the book *Outliers*, author Malcolm Gladwell talked about what is called the 10,000-hour rule. The idea is that you must practice for at least 10,000 hours in order to achieve mastery in a chosen field. I can easily tell you I spent far more than 10,000 hours being anxious and worrying. I was to anxiety what Michael Jordan was to basketball, Albert Einstein was to theoretical physics, and William Shakespeare was to writing.

I'd venture to guess that you've also spent countless hours being anxious. In fact, many people I talk to often claim they're not worried about anything specific, they simply wake up with that anxious, worrisome pit in their stomach. If this is you, congratulations! You are officially a master in the field of being anxious.

The good news is that you can use the same amount of practice that you're already doing and redirect it to new habits that will begin to change your life in a new and positive direction. It isn't a matter of work but a matter of understanding. You must become aware of how your mind works and how your actions support your behavior. Once you can see the connection behind what you do, how you think, and how you worry, you can start to take action to begin to change your behaviors, retrain your brain, and return to using your anxiety and fear in the way they were designed to be used – as a tool for focus, preparation, and awareness. Fear is not your enemy. Overuse of that fear is.

But before you can do any of that, you must first make a choice. You must choose to take action.

And I don't just mean the action to read this book. That is a good first step, but it won't magically fix your anxiety. Learning and understanding is great, but it's only part the equation.

Growing up, mixed in between my Saturday morning shows, there was a group of musical and educational cartoons called *Schoolhouse Rock*. If you grew up in the 1980s, you are probably familiar with them. If not, they were funny songs and cartoons that taught kids about English, math, science, history, and government. They were catchy tunes that would get stuck in your head, causing you to accidentally learn things. To this day, I can't hear the word "conjunction" without singing in my head, "Conjunction junction, what's your function?" (If you're still not sure what I'm talking about, Google it.)

At the beginning of each one of these songs, the intro said, "As your body grows bigger, your mind must flower. It's great to learn because knowledge is power."

And while this is something that has been echoed over and over again by many people, the idea that knowledge is power, in truth, is only partly correct. Knowledge is *potential* power. Knowing something is only powerful if you act upon your knowledge. Knowledge without action is wasted potential.

If I know how to do something, if I have the knowledge in my mind, yet I fail to act on that knowledge, I am not helping anyone or creating anything with what I know. I am not bettering myself or others simply because I know what to do in a certain situation. Only when I act upon my knowledge can I have an impact on the world around me. So the power isn't in the knowledge, but it's in the action that is taken in support of that knowledge.

If you read this book and take no action, I guarantee that nothing in this book will help you. This book contains information about what I did to overcome my anxiety. Simply listening to my stories won't cause your anxiety to dissipate. It may temporarily make you feel better, knowing you aren't alone and that other people out there understand what you are going through. But, eventually, your anxious thoughts will resurface. And unless you take new action to address them, you will continue to get the same results you've always received. You will continue to feel scared and anxious, avoid life instead of living it, and search for answers in other books, videos, and programs. You'll never find the help you need, because the solutions to people's problems are not realized in the pages of a book, but in the daily actions of the people who take what is written and put it into practice.

I want you to do an exercise with me. Get a piece of paper and a pencil. Take a moment and think about all the ways anxiety appears in your life. Write down every way anxiety has manifested itself in your life. What are the physical and emotional symptoms of your anxiety? Do you fear going into work? Do you not want to get out of bed in the morning? Are you afraid you won't be good enough for others? Are you afraid you might pass out if you go out in public? Do you worry something bad will happen to you or a loved one? How does your anxiety make you feel? How does it impact your life?

Now I want you to take that piece of paper and look at it. How many things did you write? One? Two? Ten? More?

These are all the things that are keeping you stuck in life. These are the things keeping you trapped where you are, limiting your full potential. I want you to look at this list and ask yourself one question.

Are you ready to make the choice to change your life?

If you answer yes, I want you to write down on the bottom of the paper the following: ***I will no longer allow the above items to control my life. I am ready to make a change, and I am committed to apply whatever action I need to take back my life.***

Now I want you to sign and date the paper.

This is now the contract you've signed with yourself. You know you want to make changes, and you're now committing to yourself that you'll take action. And while feeling motivated and inspired is great, willpower can only take you so far. That is why the next chapter is so important.

Because the key to making a lasting change isn't simply knowing *what* you want to change, but knowing *why*.

> *"He who has a why to live for can bear almost any how."*
> – Friedrich Nietzsche

CHAPTER 2: FINDING YOUR WHY

My parents' divorce did a number on our family – and me, in particular. It wasn't just the divorce that damaged me. Living in two houses, not waking up together as a family, and not celebrating holidays as mother, father, and children – those were obviously difficult. But what was worse was how my parents treated each other and my brother and me in the aftermath.

They hated each other. They openly fought, saying cruel insults in front of us. And when they couldn't hurt each other any more with their words, they used my brother and me as a way to inflict more pain. We became caught in the middle of their fight, and we felt powerless to stop it.

My older brother, Patrick, and I lived with our mom after the divorce. My parents sold their home, and my mother found a nice house on a lake for us. It was a great place to grow up, and I loved living there.

My dad would pick us up every other weekend to stay with him. He lived in a one-bedroom apartment about thirty minutes away. His apartment was small, so my brother and I would sleep in sleeping bags at the foot of his bed. It was kind of like camping indoors. We loved spending time with him, and we didn't care that we didn't have our own room. It was nice being close after not seeing him during the weeks we were with Mom.

Unfortunately, when my dad stopped by, my parents would always fight. It would start small – and then eventually escalate. My brother and I often got put in the middle. My mother would yell something like, "Boys, go upstairs. You're not going with your father this weekend." My father would angrily respond: "Boys, go get in the truck. We're leaving." We would sit there, not knowing what to do. Suddenly, I was three years old, standing in our old kitchen again. This same scenario played out repeatedly, well into my adult life. It was hurtful and damaging, and my parents were wrong to put us through it.

As children, we look to our parents as role models for how we will interact with the rest of the world. We pattern our behaviors, interactions, and expectations around what we learn from those who are supposed to love and care for us when we are at our most vulnerable. And while my parents never physically hurt us, the emotional scars from their words and actions left their mark.

I loved both of my parents, especially my father. I looked up to him and wanted to be just like him when I grew up.

My dad was a police officer. And even when I was young, I knew it was a dangerous job. Because I didn't see him every day, I spent countless nights lying awake, wondering if he was okay. I always worried that something would happen to him. I imagined that he might get shot, killed in the line of duty, and that I'd never see him again.

Both of my parents would try and calm my nerves by telling me nothing bad would ever happen to him and that I had nothing to worry about. But no matter what they said, I couldn't shake that overwhelming feeling of sadness and loss.

I always looked forward to the days he picked us up. It was the only time I felt comforted knowing that he was okay. I could see him, hug him, and know he was still with me. But I also felt anxious about his arrival because of how much my parents fought when he did.

This feeling of anxiety continued to grow each time my parents fought. The more they yelled, the more anxious I became. I was already a highly emotional child. I wasn't good at hiding how I was feeling. I couldn't tell a lie or mask my mood. If I was angry, I yelled. If I was upset, I would cry. This didn't serve me well if I tried to get away with anything growing up.

One time when I was little, maybe four or five years old, I had woken up early in the morning and made my way into the kitchen for a snack. I opened the refrigerator door and helped myself to a slice of cold pizza, left over from dinner the night before. Apparently, plain cheese wasn't enough of a topping for my liking, so I added a new one: cake frosting.

As I sat in the living room eating my breakfast of frosting-covered pizza, my mother came in to see what I was up to. I immediately hid the slice of pizza under the couch.

My mom looked at me and asked, "What are you eating?"

I looked up at her, my face covered in pizza sauce and frosting, and said, "Nothing."

"Steven," she said.

That was all it took. I immediately started crying.

I reached under the couch and retrieved the half-eaten pizza slice. My mother began laughing.

My life as a hardened criminal or a professional poker player was over.

This inability to control my emotions was fine when I was crying over frosting-covered pizza, but when the emotion was fear, it became a serious issue.

As I got older, my anxiety became more of a problem. School was a difficult place for me. Before each school year, I would panic about changing classrooms, changing teachers, and changing routines. I hated change. Change represented fear and panic. I already had enough change in my life. I wanted security.

As my schoolwork got more challenging, so did my anxiety.

I began to worry that I wouldn't get good grades. That I wasn't as smart as the other kids. And that I'd be singled out because of it. The more I worried, the harder it was for me to focus. My thoughts were always racing. It was as if someone had left a radio playing in the room; all I could hear was the thoughts running through my head.

I would try to study but ended up reading the same things over and over again. I could see the words and understand them, but I couldn't focus on what they meant. The voice in my head was saying, "What if you study all night and still fail? What if you're too stupid for school? What if you are the only one that fails and everyone laughs at you?"

The "what if" question was a big one for me. Everything that I did, wanted to do, or considered doing was always greeted with a string of "what ifs."

What if you can't?

What if you fail?

What if you embarrass yourself in front of everyone?

What if everyone makes fun of you?

Eventually I became so frustrated with school that I stopped trying. It gave me a feeling of being in control. If I studied and failed, it must have meant I was stupid. But if I made the choice to not study, I was failing because I chose to fail.

It sounds like bizarre logic, but in my head it made perfect sense. If I were going to fail, at least I would fail on my own terms.

I was labeled lazy by my parents and teachers. They were frustrated with me because they could see I had given up, but they didn't understand why.

The more frustrated they became with me, the more closed off I became with them. And the longer this went on, the worse it got. To them, I was a lazy kid who didn't try hard enough. In truth, I was a scared child who didn't believe in himself.

This lack of confidence and insecurity lasted for many years. Each year, the feeling seemed to get worse. I was afraid to try things or challenge myself because I didn't believe I could be successful at anything. I accepted less from others, allowed people to mistreat me, and couldn't stand up for myself – all because I thought I deserved to be treated poorly. When people treated me badly, I worked extra hard to win them over. I thought if they could love me, I might be worth something after all. I cared more about what others thought of me than of how I thought of myself. But how can someone respect you if you don't respect yourself?

People walked out of my life when they didn't need me and then walked back in when they did. I took them back because I didn't think I deserved to be treated better. I put everyone's needs ahead of my own. I clung to people who didn't want me to be strong, but needed me to stay weak. In my weakness, they became stronger. And I gave up on my dreams to simply stand next to people who wanted company as they chased theirs. My life had little value other than being there for others. Not in a good, selfless, giving-back-to-the-world way, but in a self-deprecating, unhealthy way.

I thought this was the worst of it. The path my life seemed to be on included low self-esteem and challenging relationships filled with drama and pain. I accepted this as my lot in life. I thought it couldn't get any worse.

I was wrong.

I was 22 years old when I had my first full-scale panic attack.

It was during a job interview for an entry-level design position with an ad agency. My friend's girlfriend worked there and she pulled some strings and got me an interview with the owner.

When I arrived, I was nervous. I knew I had limited experience and getting the job was a long shot at best.

As the interview began, I realized I was only half-listening to what this woman was saying. I tried to focus on her words, but the sound of my own thoughts seemed to be twice as loud as her voice. The more I strained to ignore the thoughts in my head, the louder they became.

"Why are you even here?" my mind asked in a condescending way. "You don't belong here. You can't do this."

As the stream of negative thoughts continued, I began to feel hot. My chest felt tight. It was hard to breathe. I tried to continue on, hoping it would go away.

And then it happened: A little bead of sweat started running down my forehead.

As I became painfully aware of the fact that I had started to sweat, I got more nervous. The voice in my head told me I needed to stop sweating or she was going to think there was something wrong with me. The more I worried, the hotter I got, and the more I started to sweat.

Soon, I was completely soaked with sweat. It was running down my face as if I had just finished running a marathon in the afternoon heat. It was impossible for the owner not to notice.

"Are you okay?" she asked me with a look of concern on her face. "You look like you're about to pass out. Do you need to take a minute?"

Take a minute? What I needed was to take a shower. I was drenched with sweat and completely mortified. I had never had anything like this happen to me before.

From that moment on, I had something new to be anxious about: panic attacks. I started obsessing over having them. Just the idea of a panic attack would bring one on. It became more difficult to go out and do things. The more I worried about having them, the more of them I had.

I tried coming up with coping mechanisms to deal with the panic and anxiety. I carried a bottle of cold water everywhere I went in case I started to feel warm or anxious.

I couldn't sit anywhere that made me feel enclosed or confined. I always had to sit at the end of a table or on the end of a row of seats. Whenever possible, I would sit all the way in the back, away from everyone.

Before I went anywhere or did anything, I would obsess over what might go wrong before I got there. What if the room was too hot and I started sweating? What if I got stuck sitting in the middle of a group of people? What if I have a panic attack and everyone sees?

What made the panic attacks so bad was that, for the first time, my anxiety was no longer something I could hide. It had always been a voice inside my head. It only impacted me internally. But now it was on full display for the world to see and judge. I couldn't hide it. I couldn't control the physical symptoms any more than I could control the thoughts that brought them on.

I felt like I was slowly going crazy, and I was powerless to do anything about it. I was a prisoner in my own life, and all I wanted to do was escape.

The only way to do that was to start avoiding situations all together. I began calling out sick from work. I stopped socializing with friends. I avoided going out in public.

When I couldn't avoid a situation, I used alcohol to self-medicate. I found that after having a couple drinks, my anxiety seemed a little more manageable.

Soon, I was drinking all the time.

Sadly, in our society, it's far more acceptable to have a few drinks to calm your nerves than it is to take medication for an anxiety disorder. There is a stigma attached to mental disorders. We don't like talking about them. We don't like admitting they exist, and we sure as hell don't want to acknowledge that we might have one. So I drank.

I would sneak alcohol before I would go out places, taking a shot or chugging a beer before leaving the house. I would get to places early and have a few drinks to help take the edge off before everyone got there. The truth is, the only time I felt good was when I was drunk. It gave me a break from all the voices in my head, the fear in my heart, and the pain in my life. I knew I had a problem, but I wouldn't face it. I couldn't face it. Giving up drinking meant giving up the only time I ever felt normal. If I couldn't drink, I would have nothing left that would help me not feel like me.

And the truth is, I'd rather have been seen as someone with a drinking problem than someone with a mental health problem.

But now I had both.

I saw myself as weak. I hated myself. I hated my anxiety. I hated that little voice in my head. I felt surrounded by happy people living normal lives, and I was suffering, hiding in my silence, worried someday someone would find out my secret. I wasn't normal. Something was wrong with me. And believe it or not, I had somehow managed to keep my anxiety and panic attacks hidden from almost everyone I knew. The people closest to me knew something wasn't right, but no one ever pushed to find out what.

On the outside, my life looked normal. I got married, bought a house, and had a decent job. But inside, I felt weak and scared. I had no confidence.

I was physically unhealthy from years of drinking, and I was mentally unhealthy from years of stress and worry. I had strained relationships with almost everyone in my life, including my wife, my parents, and my brothers and sister.

I lied to myself and to everyone around me that I was happy. I walked through life waiting for it to be over, but also being terrified that it might end. I was miserable, hiding behind a quirky smile and a drink.

My life wasn't supposed to turn out like this, but it had. And I was powerless to do anything about it. All I could do was keep pretending, keep moving forward, and hope for a miracle.

That miracle came on June 25, 2006.

We named her Lilianne, and she was perfect.

In the days and weeks after she was born, something shifted

inside of me. I wasn't sure what it was, but I could feel it clear as day. This perfect little person would grow up to call me Dad. That was an honor. But it also brought up a lot of feelings I had spent much of my life burying.

I had pain, anger, and resentment inside me from my childhood. Now having a child of my own, I suddenly began looking at my youth from a different perspective. I had always seen my life through my own eyes, my own perspective. I was a child, so I saw the world through the eyes of a child. But now I had one of my own. My perspective was as a parent. When I looked back at my childhood, I couldn't help but start to see things from the perspective of my parents.

As I looked at this little child, so perfect in every way, I couldn't help but feel a deep sense of love for her. I wondered if that was how my parents felt when they looked at me when I was like her. Was I ever seen as this perfect? Was I ever loved like this? If not, why? What could I have done to cause them to pull back that love from me?

I couldn't imagine my daughter ever doing anything to cause me not to love her. Maybe I hadn't done anything. Maybe I was just as perfect as she was. Maybe we all are.

My head started to swim with these thoughts, feelings, and emotions. Experiencing this shift in perspective suddenly called everything in my life into question. Had I been wrong about myself all this time? Had I been too hard on myself? Had I caused my life to end up where it was because I had believed I wasn't worthy of love, the same love I felt for my daughter with so much ease?

Maybe my parents did love me but didn't do a good job of communicating that to me. My childhood was filled with so much anger and fighting, maybe the love that was there got overshadowed. Or maybe they couldn't feel the love because they didn't feel it toward themselves, the same way I didn't feel it toward myself.

But if that was the case, was I going to do the same thing to Lili that my parents had done to me? Was I going to make her feel like she wasn't important because I didn't think I was important? Was I destined to put other people's needs ahead of what was best for her, the same way I put them ahead of what was best for me? The same way my mother and father put other people's needs ahead of mine growing up?

It was in this moment of profound clarity and understanding that I discovered something that was critical in moving my life forward. Something had been missing that kept me from being able to face and overcome my greatest fears. It kept me trapped behind a wall of anxiety and terror all the years prior to this moment.

What was missing was a reason for doing all the work, facing all the pain, and risking all the heartache. And the moment she was born, my daughter became that reason why I would fight for myself. She became the answer to the question I would ask myself every time I felt like my back was against the wall, every time I wanted to retreat in fear and give up fighting for what I believed I needed. She was the answer to the biggest question we all face when we decide to take control back in our lives: Why am I doing this?

Maybe you see yourself in my story. The facts and details may be different, but the feelings and experiences might ring true. Most people I've talked to about anxiety have similar feelings of not being strong enough or worthy enough to be happy. Their personal struggles and inner negative voice push them away from taking on the challenges of improving their life because they don't believe they can. And when things get hard, we eventually ask ourselves why am I doing this? Wouldn't it be easier to give up, stop fighting, and slip back into our old habits? The obvious answer to those questions is yes it would be easier. But in life, the easy thing to do is not always the best thing to do.

If you have a clear reason why you are doing what you are doing, you will eventually fall back into your old patterns before the new patterns have a chance to take root and grow. It will cause you to give up and retreat when things get difficult. Even when you are close to a major breakthrough, you will convince yourself you're too far away to ever reach it, and you will quit.

Quitting is easy. Giving up is safe and comfortable. Pushing through and fighting is hard. It's hard because it makes us question ourself and our actions. It opens us up to scrutiny and judgment from people around us and can make us feel vulnerable and exposed. If you are going to put yourself out there to that degree you better have a damn good reason for doing so.

Because while inspiration, motivation, and willpower are great sources of fuel, and can push you to achieve great things in life, there is only so much of it to go around. It will run out. And when it does, and that question "why am I doing this?," comes back, if you don't have a good answer, you will quit.

So how do you find the answer to "why am I doing this?" And how do you ensure that you stay on track?

Sadly, there is no one universally correct answer to this question. It is as unique as each person who asks it. My reason for doing this was my daughter. Your reason may be something completely different. Each one of us must find our own reason for going on this journey of self-awakening, self-discovery, and self-improvement. And maybe the reason you haven't begun to make these changes is because you don't know why you want to?

If you are struggling with finding your reason why, here are three questions you need to ask yourself to help put things into perspective.

Question One: What am I really afraid of?

Sit down with a piece of paper and pen, and write out all the issues you have dealt with regarding anxiety and fear. Make the list as detailed as possible. Think about how each has impacted you and limited what you've been able to do in life. Think about how each one has made you feel about yourself and about others.

Be honest, and dig as deep as you can. Don't just write, "I'm afraid of everything." That may be the case, but break it up into pieces and see where it leads you. Try to list out what it is that you're afraid might happen. If you fear being in public, what about being in public causes the fear? Is it because you're afraid of what people will think of you? If so, what exactly would that thought be? Try to be as specific as you can. The more detailed, the better.

Question Two: How will my life improve if I overcome these fears?

Now take that list, and add some positive outcomes to what would happen if you didn't have that fear. What would you do if you didn't feel limited by fear and anxiety? Would you have better relationships with others? Would you be more outgoing and maybe meet the love of your life? Would you start driving or traveling again and visit friends or family you haven't seen in years?

Again, be as specific as possible to help you get to the emotion behind the reasons.

Question Three: Why is this important?

This is the part that gives you your reason why. The answer may be obvious, or it may take a little more time. It's important to spend some time coming up with a reason that means a lot to you. It can't be something based on materialistic needs or wants, like saying, "I want to overcome my fear so I can make lots of money," because it is non-specific. What would you do with that money? Would you help your children go to college? Would you feed the homeless or give back to the community? It's the motivation behind the actions that form the basis of your reason why.

Once you have a clear idea of what your reason why is, it's time to put it to good use. Find an image or photo that best represents your reason why. It can be a picture of a person, a place, a item, or even something that just invokes an emotion or feeling inside when you look at it. Now keep that image with you at all times. When you need a motivational boost or an extra push, take the image out and remind yourself why you're doing what you are doing.

If you need a push to get up early and meditate, keep your why image next to your bed so it's the first thing you see when you wake up. When you want to roll over and go back to sleep, look at the picture and remind yourself why it's important to get up and meditate.

Knowing your why is what will keep you going no matter what you are trying to achieve. And don't simply think about your reason but actually feeling the emotional connection with it. Let the feelings associated with your reason well up inside you and inspire you to keep going. Nothing about what you are embarking on will feel natural or comfortable at first. That is why you haven't done it on your own already.

It's going to feel strange. You are going to want to quit and return to the way things were. You are going to want to feel comfortable and safe again. I can tell you from experience, when those feelings arise, it is because you are on the right track. Change doesn't feel comfortable. Comfort comes when you keep doing the same thing you always do. If you want to live a new life, you need to make new choices.

Your new life will cost you your old one.

> *"The only person you are destined to become is the person you decide to be."*
> – Ralph Waldo Emerson

CHAPTER 3: CHANGE YOUR STORY

If you're still reading this, it means you have at least begun to entertain the idea that your life needs to change. This, in itself, is a big step. Just having the awareness of what is happening is huge when it comes to learning how to overcome anxiety and negative thought patterns.

Becoming self-aware plays a major role in your ability to move forward. Being able to see what you do and why you do it with a clear understanding, rather than one that is wrapped in the ego, is key to unlocking your ability to view how you've shaped your life. For some, this might be easy. But for others, this will be incredibly difficult.

The reason this can be so hard is that some people have come to identify themselves so closely with the story of who they are that anything that challenges it – even something designed to help them

– can be seen as a threat.

When you begin to build a house, you need to start with a foundation. Everything in that house is supported by it. If the foundation is strong, the house will stand for a long time. If the foundation is weak, the house may collapse.

Our own identity is built in a similar fashion. The story we are told when we are born becomes the start of our foundation. As we get older, people we care about and trust continue to shape our beliefs, thoughts, and ideas. Based on those beliefs, we begin to look at the world and see the ideas that agree with what we already believe to be true.

It makes us feel safe and comfortable when what we see reinforces our belief. This is why we often are attracted to people with similar stories to our own. It makes us feel better when we believe we're correct. Feeling right makes us feel comfortable, safe, and stable.

For some, their desire for comfort and stability causes them to defend a flawed belief in their story for no other reason than because it's the only one they've ever known. That belief is their foundation on which they've built everything else in life. If that were to be questioned, it would call into question everything else, thrusting their entire identity into chaos and instability. This idea is so terrifying to most people that they reject it on a subconscious level. They don't know why, but they immediately – and sometimes violently – reject any notion that challenges their core belief structure.

That is why, in today's world, we find ourselves getting pulled into daily arguments via social media. A friend, colleague, or family member posts something that we don't agree with, and rather than simply respecting their opposing viewpoint, we attack their position as if they've personally offended us with their comment. Often we are not even aware of how angry we've become simply because someone else shared an idea, a belief, or a perspective that doesn't align with our own.

We respond in this way because, on a subconscious level, our ego feels threatened. We quickly reject anything that calls into question our place in the world. We want to feel safe and secure, and when that safety is threatened, we react.

I can honestly say it took me years before I realized I had a problem with anxiety. I simply thought, "This is just the way life is." Not that I thought it was normal. I always knew something was not quite right with me and the way in which I experienced the world. It was just my story and I identified with it as truth.

Most children would look up at the stars at night and see shining, bright lights that would make them "ooh" and "ahh." When I looked up at the stars, I thought about the vast emptiness of space. The idea that it continued on and on fascinated me – and it also perplexed me. How could something go on forever? Where does it go? And what is on the other side? If it exists someplace, it must exist inside something? What did space exist in and where was that? And how did it get made? Did it just appear one day? If so, what was here before space appeared?

These questions may seem deep to some or silly to others. But for me, they were all that ran through my mind each time I looked up at the stars. I couldn't just sit and enjoy the beautiful night sky the way others did. I questioned it.

This isn't a bad thing. In fact, this level of questioning led me to many of my greatest personal breakthroughs. My ability to be aware – specifically self-aware – makes all the difference in my life. The challenge has always been learning how to use that information rather than letting it scare me.

Most things that happen are not bad or good. These terms are labels we as a society have created and placed on actions so we can better incorporate them into our lives and give them meaning.

If a tree falls in the woods, it would be seen as a random action with no significant meaning. But if that tree were to fall on a hiker and cause serious injury or death, it suddenly becomes negative and tragic.

Or maybe the tree falls near the hiker, causing him to experience a near-death rush. From that sudden realization that life could end at any time, he can re-evaluate his life's direction, change careers, improve relationships with loved ones, and become a better person. Now this random act has become a motivating factor in his life to improve or change. Some would even call it fate or destiny, seeing the tree as a sign from the universe to change or wake up to true potential. Others still would see the actions of the hiker not being hit as a miraculous intervention from a higher power, protecting him from possible harm out of a deep love or compassion for life.

We as humans have a deep need to label and categorize everything we experience. We want to know how everything fits. Our lives are a great puzzle that we spend countless amounts of energy, time, and effort trying to adjust. Each experience, person, and moment become pieces that we must decide how to fit to make the picture of our life come together. Some pieces we discard because they don't seem to easily conform, while others we force into place, desperate to make them part of our story.

Our perspective of the world shapes our reality. That means we often start with the answer and make variables fit so they equal what we already want or believe to be true. Perspective is our personal and unique view of the world. No two people can have exactly the same perspective. Therefore, no two people's realities are ever exactly the same.

I will touch on this in greater detail later, but for now, you simply need to open up to the idea that the labels you place on things are uniquely dependent upon what you've experienced in life.

When I was a young child, my grandmother lived with us. She was born and raised in Paris, France. She was a little less than 5 feet tall, had big, round glasses, and white, curly hair, and she spoke with a very thick accent.

She was a fiery woman who was known for talking wildly in

French whenever she would get angry or frustrated. I would ask her what she had said, she normally responded by saying, "Nothing you should repeat!"

Over the years, she would attempt to teach me words in French. I would hold up something like an apple and ask her what it was called in French. She would say *pomme*, and I would repeat it. I remember thinking it was cool that she spoke a different language, but I also couldn't understand why she needed to. After all, an apple was called an apple. Why did anyone need a different word? Why couldn't they just call it an apple?

Because I was so young, I didn't understand that different regions of the world had their own languages well before we did. I didn't know because I hadn't experienced enough to understand time, geography, history, or the origins of languages. And because I didn't know what I didn't know, the idea that I was wrong never entered my mind. It seemed to obvious to me that an apple was called an apple, that it seemed strange that anyone would call it anything else.

My understanding of my anxiety was very much like my understanding of language. I had always had my anxiety, so it was part of me. It wasn't something I could change or do anything about. And to make it even worse, I didn't even realize I should do something about it.

I saw my negative, worrisome thinking as a necessary part of my life. It was my responsibility to be hypervigilant in every meeting, group setting, event, and all moments of my life. If I wasn't overanalyzing people, relationships, comments, looks, or opportunities, I was not being thorough. If I didn't run every negative scenario over and over again in my brain, I was somehow not doing my job as a man. I needed to be prepared. I needed to know what might happen, so I could be ready for it. If something happened and I wasn't ready, I would have failed – and I couldn't fail!

In many ways, I saw my anxiety as a responsibility. I needed to stay anxious in order to take care of myself and the people I cared about. Anxiety was how I saw the world, how I prepared for things, and how I lived my life. How could I ever go into a situation and not overanalyze everything and everyone? That would be irresponsible.

Many people see their anxiety as something they must hold on to, for many reasons. Some believe they add value to their lives by always being anxious. Others see it as just part of the person they are, unable or unwilling to change.

How many times have you heard or said the following statements:

"I'm just a nervous person."

"It's just who I am. I can't change it."

"I've always been this way."

"There's nothing I can do. This is just the way I am."

"I don't know why I'm so anxious. I just am."

These statements attempt to offer a solid reason for why anxiety has been, and continues to be, a prominent factor in a person's life. But in truth, these are examples of the negative, limiting beliefs that keep a person trapped in anxiety. This becomes the story you tell yourself and that story becomes your identity.

Most people feel as though they are powerless to deal with and overcome their anxious mind. This feeling of powerlessness is a major factor in why their anxiety is present and continuously growing. They see their anxiety as something outside of their ability to manage. Even worse, they identify themselves as *being* the anxiety. It becomes their identity as a person. To remove that anxiety would require them to lose part of who they are.

There is an old saying that if a group of people placed all their problems out on a table in front of each other with the ability to exchange their problems for another's, each person would choose to take back his or her own. Why? Because our problems are familiar to us. We are comfortable with what we know and uncomfortable with what we don't know. This is why change is so hard for people.

Change requires risking what you have for something you might not get.

My anxiety, like most people's, didn't just appear overnight. It was built over time, by many experiences, ideas, and people.

My father used to always say to me, "The devil you know is better than the devil you don't."

Now, while this statement may be true in some senses, for someone dealing with anxiety, this caused me to believe that taking a risk could make things worse.

I think this is a large driving force behind why so many people stay stuck in the same place, living the same life, and making the same choices over and over again. We develop the habit of living an anxious life. We tell ourselves the same story so many times that the story becomes who we believe we are. But is it? Are we just the collection of stories we tell ourselves, or are we more than that?

If we aren't our story, who are we?

Are we our body? Are we our mind? Are we the collection of actions we've taken, the choices we've made, or the sum of all the people we have met? Are we our family? Are we our jobs? Are we our spouse or our children's keeper?

Who do you think you are?

If you believe you are your body, let me ask you this: How much of your body can you remove and still be you? People can live missing body parts. So if you are your physical body, what part of the body makes you who you are? Is it your heart? Is it your brain? Do both need to be together in order for you to exist?

So, maybe it is the brain that makes you who you are. Then I ask this: What happens to people when they develop amnesia? Are you no longer the same person? Have you physically become someone else because you don't remember who you are?

If you are approaching the question of "Who am I?" in this manner, you are already off to a difficult start. Why? Because you are trying to solve a problem using the one part of you that fights to keep you in the dark. You are thinking about a solution when you should be feeling the solution.

Who you are is not something you can think about to find resolution. You may think about the answer to get a better understanding of who you are. But the act of thinking does not bring you to the answer, only to the question. The question "Who am I?" can be thought about forever, but never truly answered. In order to answer this question, you must "feel" for the answer within yourself. If you do this, you will discover the answer that has been there all along, like a memory, or a name on the tip of your tongue that you struggle to recall.

The closest I've come to answering this question has been through deep meditation and self-realization. It is not something that's easily put into words because it isn't something that is easy explained with the mind and our limited vocabulary. The best way to put it is to say that we are not the vehicle but the driver behind the wheel. We are not the light bulb but the electricity that makes it shine. We are not the physical body but the non-physical "self" that inhabits the body for a temporary time.

This realization is not something you can think about and know as true but rather something you must feel within yourself.

I've heard many people say as they get older, "I still feel like I'm that young kid in this older body." That feeling of being a young kid is the experience of feeling who you actually are! That is why you feel like you are the same person even though nothing physically is the same; you are the same inner energy. You can think, or remember, what it was like for you when you were that age but it is not the same as experiencing the feeling of still being that same, unchanged person.

Our bodies grow and change constantly throughout our lives. In fact, it is always changing. Cells die and are replaced by new cells, causing our entire physical structure to be replaced approximately every seven years. The baby that you were at birth no longer exists. That toddler in pictures or home movies is no longer with us. The teenager that went through high school is long gone.

You can't revisit these versions of yourself because they no longer exist.

Even our minds are not the same. The things we knew as a child – our thoughts and impressions of the world – have changed and evolved over time. We don't believe all the same beliefs as we did when we were children. Nothing about our physical being remains from when we were younger. Yet every one of us has this feeling that part of us is the same. Part of us has been there this entire time, experiencing everything. That part of us, the part that has always been there, is still there. Maybe you feel it stirring inside you right now?

Take a minute and close your eyes. Focus your attention inward. See if you can feel that inner you, that part of your being that has never changed. That part that has been there this entire time, living the life your body has been carrying it through. It is this inner feeling that is who we are. Some call it our spirit, our soul, our inner power, or our chi. Still others call this our life force or consciousness. It has no name; it has a temporary body and it is living a temporary human experience – an experience you know better as your life. It is the energy of the universe. It is part of each and every one of us, and it is who we really are. Take a minute and try to feel this.

This is a part that most people don't want to discuss or feel comfortable thinking about. It highlights our own mortality, it brings up questions about religion, God, or faith, and it makes some people close off and shut down. If you are one of those people, I would simply ask you to stay open minded to the ideas present here. This book is not about your religious beliefs. I do not ask you to question your faith or to even pick a side when it comes to religion. Personally, my spirituality is one of growing love and acceptance. You don't need to be Buddhist, Catholic, Jewish, Muslim, Hindu, or any other religion to read this book or to benefit from what it has to offer.

All I'm asking is for you to begin to open up your mind to the idea that we are only here for a temporary period of time. Our lives are very short and also very long. And part of our ability to resolve our suffering and understand the basis of our anxiety is to accept the idea that there are forces beyond our comprehension.

Some of these forces we need to confront in order to understand how they impact our subconscious mind and our attitudes about what we believe to be true.

I'm not even saying that you have to abandon your ideas or beliefs, just simply become aware of how what you believe shapes your reality.

Our story, body, thoughts, mind, and beliefs all step up to take turns as being the true self at different times in our lives. Learning to be aware of these shifts in our understanding and allowing yourself to be loosely attached – rather than firmly and permanently affixed – will allow yourself the space to examine ideas and possibilities that, until now, may have seemed foreign to you.

This book is designed to simply plant the seed of an idea. If it begins to sprout immediately, that's great. If it takes an entire lifetime, or longer, for that seed to take root, that is okay, too.

I previously wrote that many people identify with their story so closely that they'll reject anything they feel is questioning or chipping away at that truth. Much of what I'm saying in this chapter might start to make you feel uncomfortable. You might find yourself pushing away and closing off. I hope that you'll stick with it and trust that I am writing this book from a place of love and service to all those who still suffer from anxiety and fear. Our lives are beautiful experiences designed to be lived to their fullest. I want to help as many people as I can realize they are not their bodies, their jobs, their ideas, thoughts, or beliefs.

You are so much more than you even know. And the universe is just waiting for you to realize how amazing you already are.

> *"The soul becomes dyed
> with the color of its thoughts."*
> – Marcus Aurelius

CHAPTER 4: UNDERSTANDING YOUR THOUGHTS

There are two types of thought in our mind: conscious and subconscious. Conscious thought is that which is out in the open, where we have an awareness of them. This type of thinking is usually controlled, such as when we are problem-solving, attempting to recall information, or processing an action that is happening. The other type is subconscious thought. This operates in the background, and we're often unaware it is taking place. It drives us in a way we don't fully understand on the conscious level.

Have you ever had someone make a comment that upset you, but you weren't sure why you reacted so strongly? Chances are there was a subconscious thought motivating your response. You don't know why the reaction took place because you are not consciously aware of the thinking that generated it.

For almost forty years, I suffered from compulsive thinking. My mind never stopped running. I suffered. I hurt. I felt guilty, powerless, weak, fearful, and worthless – all because my thoughts made me feel this way.

I identified who I was with what I thought. To me, my thoughts were what I was, the mental representation of the person. They told my story, who I had become, and who I would always be. I thought this because my thoughts told me this was the truth. My thoughts dictated my entire life, and I seemed to have no control over them. I felt like a victim within my own body. My thoughts said things were bad in my life. They told me I wasn't good enough to achieve my goals. They reminded me of all the bad I had done and all the mistakes I had made. They made me feel horrible about who I was and convinced me that I deserved everything awful that ever happened to me.

Of course, I had no idea that I was causing this thinking myself – much like you may not believe you are causing your thinking, either. Most of what I thought came from my experiences with the outside world. Things my parents, my friends, and even the world said or did is what caused me to think and feel this way, right?

I believed others caused this pain in me, so naturally I blamed everyone else for how I felt. I blamed the outside world for being so hard. My parents, for not raising me in a more loving and supportive home. My friends, for not understanding me or asking if I was okay when I was clearly not okay growing up. I blamed school for being too demanding, my partners for being too selfish, and the pressures of society for making me feel like I would never be enough. I even blamed God for not fixing it and making it all better.

I blamed everyone and everything for how I felt on the inside. But the truth is, how you feel on the inside comes from the inside. You may be reacting to the outside world but that reaction is an internal one, not external. How you respond to the world dictates how you feel. The external world is not for or against you. You make it so by what you believe.

But at this point in my life, I had no idea that's how it worked, nor would I have believed you if you had told me – much like many of you might be saying "bullshit" to me right now. It's okay if you feel the world is pushing you around. It's okay if you feel a bit out of control. But all I ask is that you start to open up to the idea that maybe you have more control over how you react than you believe you do. If you can do that, you'll be able to absorb what comes next.

The reason I didn't believe it at the time was because my thoughts narrated my every move. From the moment I woke up in the morning until the time I fell asleep, thoughts ran through my head with little regard for the damage they were doing to my self-esteem, psyche, relationships, or my life. I suffered from severe depression and anxiety, all because I had fallen victim to the greatest mistake we can make. I believed *what I thought was who I was*.

Ironically, it was through a random set of circumstances – if you believe in such things – that I was brought to my most profound teaching in life. And it all came from watching a Jim Carrey video.

Yes, you heard me correct. The star of movies like *Ace Ventura, Pet Detective*, *Dumb and Dumber*, *The Mask*, and *Me, Myself and Irene* somehow would become my spiritual guru, leading me to a teaching that would change my life forever.

I was spending the afternoon much like I normally did, surfing Facebook as a way to distract myself and avoid doing any meaningful work in, or on, my life. A friend of mine posted a video of the funnyman that I happened to click on. It didn't seem like his normal video clips, contorting himself in unrealistic positions, making funny voices, and acting insane for others' amusement. This video was different.

In it, he stood stoic, dressed all in black. A large blue screen was behind him. As he began speaking, I was mesmerized by his words. There was sincerity behind what he spoke that I found hypnotic.

I woke up and I suddenly got it. I understood suddenly how thought was just an illusory thing. And how thought is responsible for, if not all, most of the suffering we experience. And then I suddenly felt like I was looking at these thoughts from another perspective. And I wondered, 'Who is it that's aware that I'm thinking?' And suddenly I was thrown into this expansive, amazing feeling of freedom. From myself. From my problems. I saw that I was bigger than what I do. I was bigger than my body. I was everything and everyone. I was no longer a fragment of the universe. I was the universe. And ever since that day… I've been trying to get back there! It comes and it goes. It's like riding a wave. Sometimes I'm on and sometimes I'm off. But at least I know where I want to go. And I want to take as many people with me as I possibly can. Because the feeling is amazing.

I had no idea what he was talking about at the time, but his voice and his words connected with me on a deep and spiritual level. I needed to know more. I needed to learn more.

So I began searching for Carrey online, looking for other speeches he had given or, at the very least, a full version of what he had said. Eventually I found the source of the video: It was from 2009 for an event for the Global Alliance for Transformational Entertainment, introducing author Eckhart Tolle. I had no idea who this person was, so I began researching his name as well. I learned he had written a couple of popular books on spirituality and had even been featured by Oprah Winfrey. I was surprised that I had never heard of him before, and I was intrigued.

I left work that afternoon and, rather than heading home, I stopped by the local bookstore and picked up a copy of his book, *The Power of Now*. I went home that night and began reading.

In his book, Tolle wrote about many topics but the one that struck me the most was the idea of being the "watcher of your thoughts." He wrote about how his own thoughts had become too much for him to live with. He openly stated, "I cannot live with myself anymore." As he made this proclamation, he was struck by the idea that "If I can't live with myself, who is the self I cannot live with? Are there two of me?"

I finished his book and decided to do something I hadn't done since I was a young man. In an attempt to help manage my anger, my father enrolled me in martial arts classes. (I know it may sound strange to take a child with anger issues and teach him how to fight, but it has long been proven that studying martial arts instills a respect for discipline and control. It absolutely did with me.)

As part of our practice, we would begin and end every class with meditation. It was a chance to sit, quiet the mind, and focus simply on our breathing. I had not done this for many years. The truth was, I didn't like the quiet. My thoughts overwhelmed me when it was quiet. In fact, for most of my life, I had to sleep with either a television or radio on because I couldn't rest without noise. When there was silence, my mind seemed to be at its loudest.

Feeling inspired by this book, I decided to brave the quiet of my room. I lay in my bed with the intention of listening to my thoughts. I was simply going to observe everything I was doing, thinking, and feeling with absolute focus. I used all my senses. I noticed the sheets of the bed touching my skin, the temperature of the room and how it felt on my face, the hum of the fan that was running in my room, the noises outside like the neighbor's dog and the wind in the trees.

I also started to feel the sensations within my own body. I focused my thoughts on the feeling of my feet and lower legs. I noticed, when I focused my attention on that part of my body, I could feel what is best described as a tingling or buzzing there. The more I focused on this feeling, the stronger it became.

As I continued this process, I suddenly came to a realization: I wasn't thinking at all! No thoughts were going through my mind! The voice that had been narrating my entire life back to me, that voice that I didn't seem to be able to control, was suddenly silent. Of course, it was silent only until I became aware it was silent. At the very moment I placed my awareness on my thinking, I was suddenly thinking again. But now, something was different. I wasn't just thinking, I was now aware I was thinking – and then it happened! Suddenly, I was watching my thoughts. I had found that place where I could feel the experience of being aware of my thoughts, without actually being them.

It was in that moment of awareness, for the first time, that I experienced the present moment. The very moment I existed in time and space. I was aware that I was aware, not through thought but through feeling. I suddenly became conscious! This was when I woke up to the idea that I was not my thoughts, actions, mistakes, sins, fears, or even my physical body. All of those things were part of the experience I was aware of, but they were not who I was. I was the awareness, the consciousness.

The strangest part of it all was how familiar it felt. It was as if I hadn't learned something new, but rather I had remembered what I had forgotten!

I suddenly understood what being the watcher of my thoughts meant. It meant actually being aware, being conscious. I was now watching everything, including how my mind responded to the physical world around me. I was not my thoughts: I was the awareness of my thoughts. I was the one watching them. I was not the physical form but the non-physical consciousness.

My thoughts were connected to the physical world. Past experiences, future possibilities, and present observations made up all of my thoughts. But when I was aware, I wasn't thinking. I was experiencing just being. This allowed me to view my thoughts as the observer. This crystal-clear understanding of not being the physical form, but the non-physical formless, suddenly freed me from my thoughts.

That night, I drifted off effortlessly to sleep – something I had rarely done before. Normally, the chatter in my mind would keep me up for hours. But this night, I could almost feel myself slipping seamlessly from an awakened state into blissful slumber.

When I awoke the next morning, the experience of being the observer of my thoughts was still very fresh in my understanding. I almost felt as if I were a passenger within my own body, looking down on myself but still somehow simultaneously inside.

As I got out of bed, I felt the carpet beneath my feet. It felt warm, fuzzy, and tickled a bit. I had walked on this carpet thousands of times before, but this was the first time I could really feel it under my feet.

Normally as I got out of bed, my only thoughts were about what I had to do at work, how I needed to hurry so I wouldn't be late, or how I didn't really even want to get up in the first place. My mind had always been so loud and so busy projecting itself into the future, I never left space to be in the moment I was in. It was as if I was standing on my feet, on that carpet, and feeling it for the first time without being distracted.

As I walked across my house and entered the bathroom, the lights and colors seemed to be amplified in some way. Everything was much brighter and sharper. I got into the shower and could feel the water running down my body. I looked at the drips of water as they ran down the shower curtain. The pattern on the curtain was a fine, white-on-white crisscross pattern. As each drip ran down the curtain, I could see the pattern bow and distort through the lens of the water drop. It was a level of detail I'm not sure I'd ever experienced before, and it was amazing.

Without the loud, distracting voice narrating my fears and worries, I was able to see what was happening as it was happening. I was consciously aware of my surroundings without having to think about them. In fact, as the narration began, I became aware of it and could listen as if I was eavesdropping on someone else's conversation. It was strange and wonderful all at the same time.

For the next few months, I had what I like to call my "inner-body experience." I walked around in a state of wonder. I saw things differently than I ever had before, and I suddenly felt freer than I had ever imagined. I saw the world as a place to play, not a place to fear or worry about. I no longer saw everything simply through my physical eyes, but through a lens of awareness. The universe became a wondrous place, filled with the most amazing people and endless possibilities.

I also became aware of how much our current world and people don't understand this way of being. Almost everything we are taught pushes us to conform to a way that keeps us prisoner to our thoughts and our ego. The world focuses on the physical because it believes that's all there is. We feel we are physical beings who can only find happiness through other physical accomplishments. We use money, power, fame, food, drink, drugs, relationships, and other physical elements to create happiness for ourselves. But once we start to look inside, we realize that the outer world is simply a reflection of what we feel inside. We create our reality through our feelings, not the other way around.

By obtaining a state of awareness, it is far easier to realize the truth about our lives. The truth is, we are here to play, live, love, and experience all that life has to offer. The universe is not here to help or to hurt us, but to serve us as we ask to be served. We've simply forgotten how to ask for what we want.

This experience allowed me to feel for the first time the reality that I am not my thoughts, just as you are not your thoughts. Your thoughts are happening in your head, within your mind, but it is not who you are.

Let me repeat that for emphasis: *You are not your thoughts!*

Who you are is the awareness that the thought is there. You are the one listening to those thoughts. This is the truth that we all must come to in order to begin this journey. We must connect with our inner consciousness. Our true self is that which is aware of the self.

The more aware we become of our thoughts, the more conscious awareness we can bring to our thoughts. The less aware we are, the more we allow our subconscious thoughts to run our lives. For most people, subconscious thought is responsible for almost all of their actions and reactions to the world. The choices they make about their friends, what food to eat, what job to do, and what opinions to hold most important feel as though they come from conscious thought. However, if we really focus our attention on why we are choosing what we choose, we can become aware that these decisions are driven by the subconscious mind. Thus, we can consciously make another choice.

When we live from the subconscious mind, we function as if we are on autopilot. We get up, get dressed, go to work, come home, have dinner, watch television, and then go to sleep. Because our lives run from this subconscious state, we often have very little awareness of what we are doing from moment to moment. The more we live in this subconscious state, the more we listen to our mind narrate what we are already doing rather than fully understanding the motivation behind why we are doing it, thus creating the illusion of control. If I'm doing something, I must be doing it because I am choosing to do so.

Picture your thought as if it is a computer. Your subconscious is the programming that's running in the background. This program is designed to collect and categorize data, determine how it is useful to the system, store this data, and recall it when necessary. It is designed to run constantly, quickly, and efficiently – so much so that we become unaware that the program is running at all. As a result, we eventually lose the perspective of who we are in relationship to the system. We allow the program to convince itself that it is in control. In order to avoid this from happening, we must be aware of the fact that our thoughts are simply data running in the program of our mind.

When we live from a state of believing we are our thoughts, we create great suffering for ourselves. Our thoughts serve to distract us from who we truly are by keeping our focus on things that are not happening right now. They make us feel as if the thought is happening currently, but all thought is an illusion. Thoughts focus on either the past or the future, not the present moment. We must learn to quiet our thoughts of the past and future so we can open up to the beauty and reality that is our present lives. Living within the moment we are given is far more meaningful, productive, and satisfying. Living in the past causes us to focus on pains and regret. Even when the memories of the past are what we would consider to be happy memories, they can bring about a longing for what once was rather than celebrating what is.

For the average person, thoughts of the future tend to be of a nervous, fearful nature. Looking to what might be should cause us to be optimistic and excited for what today's endeavors will produce. Instead, they tend to cause us to worry about what might happen, causing stress and anxiety in our current lives. This stress lessens the quality of our current moment, ensuring that we cannot build a better tomorrow.

Please don't get me wrong. I am not saying that we should never reflect on the events of the past, think about our futures, or make plans for what we want to achieve. Planning and reflection are incredible tools for creating the life you want. How else can you create and grow if you never put yourself in a place to be given the opportunity to do so? That takes thought and planning. Your mind is designed exactly for this purpose and should be used as such. The problem is that we have become so out of touch with our inner self that we've begun living our lives as if we are our minds and thoughts, rather than simply using them as tools to create and experience the lives we desire. In other words, use your mind or your mind will use you.

Where your thoughts lead, your life will follow. It is time to stop letting your thoughts lead you down a path of fear, anxiety, worry, sorrow, guilt, depression, and anger. We must all learn to get back in touch with who we truly are. We are not the physical mind or body, but the non-physical spirit, soul, and energy inside. In order to take back control of the vehicle, we must relearn we are not the vehicle but the pilot, and we are at the controls.

A Simple Meditation Practice

For many people, meditation is a scary and misunderstood practice. People think they must learn specific ways or mantras that must be repeated in order to unleash a mystical and unrealistic sense of enlightenment. I'm here to dispel that myth right now. Any meditative practice can work, it simply depends on what works best for you. Some people can simply focus on their breath. Other people enjoy guided meditation where they can focus on the voice of another person as they focus their minds. Still others reach a meditative state while doing physical activity like yoga, walking, running, playing a musical instrument or even cleaning. Meditation is simply a way of sharpening your focus and teaching your mind to relax and observe without processing and judging.

To get you started, here is my simple meditation practice I use every day. Feel free to research other forms of meditation that may be more to your liking. The key, no matter which type of meditation you practice, is to do it each day.

1.) Find a quiet, relaxing place to either sit or lie down. It can be on the floor, seated in a chair, or on a cushion – whatever makes you feel most comfortable.

2.) Set a timer for whatever amount of time you think you can sit in silence. Start small and slowly work up to twenty minutes if you can.

3.) Relax your muscles. If you are seated, let your shoulders drop and allow your body to sink into the chair or floor.

4.) Breathe in through your nose. As you do, focus on the breath as it enters your nose and fills your lungs. Try to "feel" your breathing rather than "think" about your breathing. It's a subtle difference but one you'll notice when you start practicing meditation. If you feel like you are narrating inside your head, you are thinking. Just let the thoughts go and focus on "feeling."

5.) Breathe out through your mouth. Again, focus on feeling your breath as it leaves your body. As you exhale, relax even further. Feel your body "sink" into the chair or floor with each breath.

6.) Do this twice a day, once in the morning and once in the evening. You can also do this any time you feel stressed and anxious.

If you find you are having trouble quieting your mind, try repeating the phrase "I am" as you breathe. In your mind, say "I" as you inhale. Say "am" as you exhale. This will help focus your mind and allow you to better relax.

The key is to start small. While it is often recommended to meditate for twenty minutes at a time, this can feel like an eternity for some people. Meditation is a skill that takes time to learn. You wouldn't expect to walk into a gym after never working out, jump on a treadmill and run for ten miles, would you? Your mind and your body work the same way. Don't expect pure enlightenment the moment you sit down. Creating unrealistic expectations is the exact opposite of what you are trying to accomplish through meditation. Ease your mind into the practice and give yourself room to struggle.

For beginners I often suggest starting out with just sixty-seconds of watching your breathing few times throughout the day. After you feel comfortable with that, expand the time by another minute until you work your way up to a longer amount of time.

The reason I love this simple breathing meditation is because it helps to train my body to respond to my breathing by relaxing.

Each time you slow your breathing and relax your body you are telling your body that this is how should respond. You create a cause-and-effect link in your brain that will make it easier to relax when you become stressed. The more you practice linking your breathing with your body relaxing, the easier it will be to calm yourself when you feel stressed or anxious.

This is a great practice for those who suffer from anxiety or panic attacks because you can use this exercise to combat the anxious 'rush' you feel when stressed. As you begin to feel anxiety and stress rise, take a moment and remind yourself to breath while returning your focus to your breath. Your body will recognize this as a sign to relax and allow you to reduce your anxiety over time. The more you practice meditation the quicker your body will to respond to the breathing.

Just remember that practice is the key. Don't expect to meditate in the morning and have your anxiety disappear by lunch. Anxiety and stress is a practiced behavior that you've already become efficient at. Allow yourself the time to build new and healthier habits in your life. Be patient with yourself. You will get there eventually.

"The real meditation practice is how we live our lives from moment to moment to moment."
– Jon Kabat-Zinn

CHAPTER 5: LIVING MINDFULLY – BECOMING PRESENT

One of the most amazing realizations I have made in my recovery and discovery travels has been awakening to the mindful appreciation for the present moment. Simply the introduction to the idea of being mindful has been an eye-opening and earth-shattering revelation.

For the better part of thirty years, I was not present for events that took place in my life. All the parties, celebrations, family dinners, holidays, vacations – I was barely present for any of them. Not because I wasn't physically there, but because I wasn't mentally there. I was there in body but not in mind or awareness.

My anxiety kept me in a constant state of fear, stress, and worry. I projected my attention onto the future moments of each event, always vigilantly watching for what dangers or problems might arise within the upcoming moments of my day. I looked forward, wondering, fearing, and never fully allowing the awe, brilliance, or beauty of my life to be fully appreciated.

I was there for my life, but I was not present. This is the great sadness I have looking back over my life: knowing how much I missed the details of my world because I was too fearful of them not rising to my expectations or too worried they would fall to meet them.

My life has been a series of painful dramas, unfortunate circumstances, and regrettable failures – and most of them never truly happened. I lived in a negative world of my own creation and imprisonment. Like an inmate locked in a jail cell, I never realized I held the key to my own freedom. My eyes could never see that key because it was only visible in the present moment, viewed by those mindfully aware of its existence.

I didn't know this place existed, this present moment. I had heard the words before, to be present and be mindful. Most people hear this and have no idea what it means. The idea of being mindful was just some nonsense phrase with no practical purpose or meaning to me. It wasn't real. It wasn't something that was any different from how we all lived every day. Of course we were present, where else would we be? I'm here because that's where I am. I can't be any other place. If I could, I probably would be.

Most of the time I hated where I was. I hated *who* I was.

My present moments were spent asking myself why I got stuck with this life. Why did I have to suffer when so many other people seemed happy? What were they doing that I wasn't? Why couldn't my life be more like theirs? What had I done to deserve all this? So many people had done far worse things than I had, yet they seemed to be living fun, enjoyable lives while I was left fearing every interaction, every conversation, and every public encounter.

Be present? I wanted to be anywhere but where I presently was. Be mindful? All I could hear was my mind.

My mind never stopped talking, never stopped worrying, never stopped reminding me of who I was, where I was, and what I was. Why would I want to put *more* focus on that?

Aren't we all already present in our lives? Aren't we all mindful of what is going on? To me, it seemed more like the problem than the solution. I wanted to be less present in my life. I wanted to have anyone else's life *but* my own. I didn't want to be mindful of things because I thought they were already so bad. Being present and mindfully aware was the one thing I thought I needed *less* of!

After all, if I'm not in the present moment, where am I? Am I a time traveler who's living in the past or visiting the future?

As it turned out, that was exactly what I was doing. I was time traveling.

One of my favorite movies is *Back to the Future*. If you are the one person who's never seen the movie, it's about Marty McFly, a teenager whose best friend, a scientist named Dr. Emmett Brown, turns a DeLorean car into a time machine. He ends up going back to when his parents first met and accidentally interferes with that meeting, endangering his own existence. Marty spends the rest of the movie trying to get his parents back together so that their future – and his – isn't altered.

This movie, along with almost all other time-travel stories, seems to have the same warning attached to it: It's the idea that time travel can have disastrous effects on the present.

I can tell you firsthand that time travel is possible, and, yes, it has disastrous effects on the present moment.

Many people time travel all day, every day, just with their minds rather than with their bodies. Most of the time, our minds are either focused on an event, experience, or regret from the past or keeping a fearful eye on something that may take place in the future. Most people are so consumed with the past and the future that they are missing the only moment that truly exists. That moment is right now, the present moment.

No time exists other than the present moment – at least, no

time we are currently experiencing. We can only experience things right now. There is no past. Past is simply a present moment that has already gone by. There is also no future, at least not the way we think of it. We tend to see the future as something that will happen to us later on. But that later only exists in relationship to now. We will never reach the future because when we do, it is experienced as the present now.

This moment, right now, is that future you envisioned yesterday. But it does not feel like the future, does it? It feels like right now. Nor does it feel like the past. It will be viewed as the past when you think about this moment tomorrow.

Think of it like an old filmstrip. When I was in school in the late 70's and early 80's we didn't watch movies in class on a smart-screen, on smart phones, on computers, DVDs or even VCR players. We had actual filmstrips that would be played on a projector. The film, which was simply a series of transparent images strung together, would be pulled from one reel to another, past a light and lens, which magnified and project the images on a screen or blank wall. As the images moved in quick succession it created the illusion of movement and the movie came to life on the screen.

If you were to pause the filmstrip you would see only a single image on the screen. That image on the screen is what is happening right now in the present moment. The images right before are the future and the images after are the past. As the movie plays, the individual images between past, present and future blur and become unclear. But when you take a step back you can clearly see which part of the movie has already been played and which part is yet to come. We experience our lives like the filmstrip — through a projector powered by time, experiencing moment after moment, image after image, as they pass through our light and are brought into clarity by our lens.

Each person is living their own unique life, impacted by what they've personally observed, so they naturally develop their own lens and perspective on how they see their world. It is this perspective that will either expand or limit your experience and vision of things and people around you, causing your reality to be either full of positive opportunities or negative pitfalls.

Our perspective works to shape our reality just as much as our reality works to shape our perspective. It all depends on how aware we are that this interaction is taking place. If we are not fully focused on all the elements that go into creating our perspective, how can we be fully present in what we are experiencing? When we narrow our perspective focus to train on a specific element, feature, or experience, we distort all other elements we are experiencing, causing some to advance into the foreground and others to recede – or be removed altogether. This can also be summarized by saying we see what we want to see, or, more accurately, we see what we expected to see.

When we focus our attention on all the negative things we fear might happen, everything we experience is seen through the lens of how it might endanger us, cause us pain, inflict suffering, or fall short of our expectations. We train our mind to see the things we believe to already be there, thus improving our ability to find it and prove ourselves correct. Very rarely do we ever enter into a situation with little to no expectation as to how things will turn out.

How often have you reacted to an experience by saying, "I knew that was going to happen" or "I didn't see that coming"? In both cases, you entered the situation with an expectation of how you believed things would turn out. Thus, your experience either matched or didn't match what you were looking for. When events meet our expectations, we feel good. When they don't, we suffer. The expectation becomes part of our perspective even before we experience or witness what is about to take place.

When we become more mindful of our thoughts and feelings, we become more aware of the perspective that we bring to each event in our lives. We can see how we are shaping our experiences even before they happen. The deeper you can go into your awareness, the more you realize that much of what you do, say, and experience is coming from a deeply ingrained programming of your subconscious mind that controls how you experience your life.

Everything we've experienced, seen, heard, been taught, and believed is part of this programming. And like so much of our subconscious mind, it is often running in the background without any conscious involvement or control. When we learn to become more aware of this push and pull by our subconscious mind, we can start to witness the behind-the-scenes influences, interrupt the automatic response, and put ourselves back into the conscious driver's seat of our own lives.

But the first step in doing this is simply to become aware of how much of our lives we've given control over to our subconscious mind and perspective. And this can be achieved by practicing mindfulness.

So how do we do this? How can we learn to focus on the present moment and become more mindful? Often, the largest obstacle comes from our own mind. Constant, habitual, uncontrollable thought often keeps us so distracted that we're unable to fully experience the present moment. As thoughts run through our minds, they cause us to focus on either the past or the future. The more we allow our mind to think random, uncontrolled thoughts, the more we lose our connection with right now. Experiencing the present moment is more about feeling the moment than it is thinking about it. Once thoughts enter the situation, we often lose our focus and end up going down the rabbit hole of our thoughts.

In Buddhism, this is called the monkey mind. If you ever watch monkeys swinging around in the trees, they seem to be moving randomly all over the place. They jump from branch to branch, tree to tree, moving in many directions with little rhyme or reason. Our minds are very much like those monkeys, but instead of jumping from connected branch to connected branch, our mind jumps from connected thought to connected thought.

Has someone ever said something that caused you to blurt out a response that seemed completely unrelated, but in your mind there was a series of thoughts that connected the seemingly unrelated items together? You then go through the process of trying to explain the thoughts that led from the original comment to your response, only to receive stares of confusion.

I like to think of our minds like a new puppy. They are energetic and often running all over the place. One second, it's licking your face, the next it's chasing a ball, and then it's trying to catch its own tail. Puppies are cute and lovable, so it's forgivable when they pee on the floor, chew up your favorite shoe, or slobber all over your aunt when she comes for a visit.

But as that puppy gets older and bigger, if it is never trained how to behave, its wild, undisciplined actions quickly go from fun and lovable to disruptive and obnoxious. Our minds are very much like puppies that have never been trained. They are all over the place with very little discipline and no focus on what they are or are not supposed to be doing at any given moment.

You can send puppies to a trainer or an obedience school, where they are taught through a series of repetitive actions about discipline, rules, boundaries, limitations, rewards, affection, and their role in the pack or family. But for most of us, no such trainer or school exists for our mind. Our mind usually is left to fend for itself. The only training our mind ever gets is through education. But in most cases, this process is simply teaching it about facts and figures that it must memorize and regurgitate in order to pass a test. As we get older, we learn skills designed around doing a job or accomplishing a task. We are more often taught *what* to think rather than *how* to think. And the other areas of our mind that are designed around rewards, affection, boundaries, and limitations are left untrained and undisciplined. Our minds simply learn to react to the stimuli that they experience through chance, repetition, and exposure to other like minds that also were never fully trained or disciplined.

In many ways, our minds are like packs of wild dogs running around uncontrollably, doing whatever they feel like at any given moment. The only discipline used as forms of control are the legal, moral, or religious boundaries that are placed around the actions we take in society. But even these don't often work as a proper deterrent, given the number of crimes committed each year, the wars that take place, and the amount of suffering we endure that cause people to overmedicate and underappreciate the lives they live. Regardless of the personal or professional success some achieve, they still feel unsettled, uneasy, and incomplete. Their minds have them searching for things that are not there, creating goals that are unattainable and desiring rewards that are unrewarding.

It has been my experience that this is due to the poor and/or nonexistent training we offer for our minds. We are blessed with the most powerful tool in the human body, and we have no idea how to train it. Or we are unaware of the training we have available to us. For me, that training is the art of meditation and the daily practice of mindfulness.

Through meditation, we can learn to interact with our mind, using it as a tool rather than allow it to use us. By including a regular meditation practice in our daily lives, we can learn to witness our thoughts as things that are pushing and pulling our desires. With this awareness, we're able to consciously choose which thoughts we engage with and which ones we allow to pass by. We can build boundaries and limits to what we allow the mind to control in our lives. We can also use those same powerful thoughts to motivate, inspire, and visualize things that truly serve us as individuals and as a collective consciousness. And if meditation is the process of training your mind to slow down and process thoughts in a new and more efficient way, mindfulness is how that training is implemented in your daily life.

The act of being mindful is very simple. But like most things I've learned on this journey, simple doesn't necessarily mean easy. Being mindful is often a hit-or-miss activity. The times when my meditation and mindfulness practices are all in sync, I feel as if my body, mind, and soul are all in perfect harmony. I see things clearly, and I'm able to witness so much of the world without attachment, without fear or worry. It is a mystical place that I find myself in awe of, never wanting to leave.

But these moments of bliss can last for mere flashes of a second, disappearing as quickly as they appeared. The more I try to hang on to the feeling, the quicker it seems to fade away. The more I search for it, the more it alludes me. I have found that it is the trying that keeps me from succeeding and the wanting that keeps me from having. And this is why the discipline of the mind is so important to develop. Because the speed in which our thoughts can betray us requires a constant vigilance and dedication that, at first, can seem exhausting. But in truth, it is only exhausting because it is so new. Anything you try to learn for the first time is extremely difficult. People don't become experts after the first try. Especially not something like this!

Everything in our culture is designed to pull at our attention. Our lives are designed for distraction. This is because we have lived for so long with untrained and undisciplined minds. The only break we ever get from our anxious, never-ending thinking comes in the form of distractions.

According to the website statista.com, over two billion people around the world have access to a smartphone or similar device[1]. In the United States alone, sixty-four percent of the population has a smartphone. We've become obsessed with the distraction of technology. We spend our days texting, tweeting, and sharing our pictures, stories, thoughts, and opinions. We spend even more time consuming that same information from our friends, family, and celebrities. Many of us visit social media sites before we get out of bed. For some people, their smartphone is the first thing they see in the morning and the last item they see at night.

Each time we post an update online or text message a friend,

---

[1] "Number of smartphone users worldwide from 2014 to 2020 (in billions)," Statista.com, accessed March 22, 2017, https://www.statista.com/statistics/330695/number-of-smartphone-users-worldwide/.

we wait in anticipation for the response. When it is received, a quick chemical shot of dopamine is released, triggering the reward center of the brain and causing us to want to repeat the behavior. Again, our mind is in control, and we are completely unaware it is happening.

Before smartphones, we distracted ourselves with television, radio, newspapers, magazines, billboards, and even the gossip of our friends and coworkers. We drink to forget our problems, we take medication to forget our pains, and we participate in unhealthy or unsafe behavior because it makes us feel alive, even if it's just for a brief moment.

Don't get me wrong. I'm not saying that all technology or forms of communication are bad or evil. To the contrary, it's incredibly valuable and beneficial for millions of people around the world. But much like our own minds, the way in which we use these resources greatly affects the positive or negative impact they have on our lives.

When we learn to use these in a mindful state, it is much easier to navigate the world and not get caught up in the unimportant aspects of what is available for our mental consumption. Technology has offered up an all-you-can-eat buffet of information, education, and entertainment. Healthy choices help dictate how healthy our minds stay.

Being mindful of how the information you consume impacts your mood, your emotions, and your state of mind will allow you to recognize when it's time to take a break or adjust what it is you are consuming. Without this awareness, we can and do make ourselves sick with overconsumption of negative resources.

So how do we go about learning to be more mindful? How do we experience living in the present moment? It's simple, really. Our body is designed to experience it. We need to practice shifting our focus from our thoughts back to the tools designed to keep us present and connected with our surroundings. These tools are the five senses: touch, smell, taste, hearing, and sight.

Mindful touching

The sense of touch is a great way to learn how to stay mindful and connected to the present moment. We are touching things all the time, and things are always touching us. We have a tendency to think of touch only in regards to using our hands, but if you think about it, the majority of our body is in contact with items all the time.

The clothing we wear is constantly touching our body. Our socks, shoes, pants, shirts, jackets, and hats come into contact with our skin on an almost-constant basis, but we hardly ever take the time to feel those sensations. The materials, textures, fabrics, temperature, and weight of these materials can all be used as a reminder of the present moment.

If you close your eyes and rub your hand against your shirt or pant leg, you can feel the different bumps and details of the material against your skin. Take a moment and try to visualize in your mind the texture of what you feel. Does it feel rough and offer resistance as you pass your fingers over the fabric? Is it smooth, allowing your hand to almost float with ease? Is it cool to the touch, or can you feel the heat of your body through the clothing and radiating into the nerves of your fingers and hand?

Each one of these sensations, as you allow your mind to focus on them, brings you into a more connected state of being present. Some of you may experience thoughts that come into your mind. Maybe you have a flash of a thought that this is stupid. What if someone sees me rubbing my hand on my shirt or pants? If this happens, don't judge the thought or yourself for having it. Just try to gently return your attention to the feeling of your skin touching your clothes.

This practice doesn't have to be done with clothing only. It can also be used as a great way to be more intimate with yourself or your partner. Learning to mindfully touch yourself or your partner's body can be an even more arousing experience. Even in these moments of pleasure, we can find ourselves getting lost in thought. If you are alone, you may wonder if this is wrong or what would people think if they found out you were touching yourself. If you are with your partner, you might wonder if he or she is enjoying it. Oftentimes, issues of performance anxiety arise from a mental block due to the overthinking regarding performance or inadequacy. When we get lost in our own thoughts, it can be difficult to allow yourself to become fully aroused, which can lead to issues with your partner. This can also create issues for your partner as well, if he or she begins to believe they are no longer sexually attractive to you. The problem of overthinking can have drastic and permanent implications on a relationship if not addressed.

When you use mindfulness to connect with yourself or your partner, you allow the touch sensation to remain the focus and cause the thoughts to fade into the background. When the thoughts do arise, try to direct them towards focusing to create a mental description of what you are feeling rather than of something that might distract you and remove you from the present moment. And there is nothing sexier than knowing the person you are with is giving you their undivided attention, especially in the bedroom.

Mindful smelling

The sense of smell can be a great way to mindfully connect with your surroundings. In fact, smell has a strong connection with your mind and can trigger memories you've completely forgotten about.

For years when I was a child, my family would have cookouts. It was one of the few times I remember us all being together and enjoying ourselves as a family. To this day, when I smell burgers and hot dogs on the grill, my emotional state immediately returns to that sense of happiness that I felt as a child on those warm summer afternoons in my backyard. In fact, for a long time, I struggled with my decision to become a vegetarian for this exact reason. It turned out that it wasn't the taste of the food I found myself longing for but the memories that the smell represented to me that caused my cravings. After years of practicing mindful awareness, I was able to connect the smell with that memory. This unlocked the understanding that I wasn't actually hungry for the burger but for the love and affection of that memory.

So when people say to stop and smell the roses, I recommend you take this quite literally. Physically stop and smell those roses every once in a while. Take some time and smell everything around you. Each morning, when I make myself coffee or tea, I pause and take a deep, long inhale of the smoky aroma of the coffee beans or the sweet scent of my lemon tea. There are so many textures and levels to the scent of different foods, flowers, perfumes, and just about everything else around us. Learning to pause and take that breath can be a quick reminder to be more mindful.

I recommend you take five minutes right now and find something around you that you can close your eyes and smell. Try to visualize the different parts of the aroma you are experiencing. Don't judge or attempt to describe with words what it is you smell. Simply take it in and feel the smell throughout your entire being. The moment you feel lost in that smell is the feeling of being mindfully present.

Mindful tasting

There are so many amazing benefits to eating and tasting your food in a more mindful way. So many of us inhale our food as if someone was going to come along and steal it from us. There is a whole host of negative effects from eating in this manner, both mental and physical. Not only are you not taking the time to savor and enjoy your meal, you also don't give your stomach ample time to communicate with your mind when you are no longer hungry.

They say it takes about twenty minutes for the chemical reaction caused by putting food in your stomach to reach your brain and say it's no longer hungry. If you are like most people, you probably consume far more food than is necessary to fill your stomach in that time. By slowing down, you allow your mind to recognize it is no longer hungry, causing you to eat less food.

By going slower, it also allows you to better taste the food you are eating. Chewing your food for longer amounts of time and allowing your taste buds to take in the flavors and textures of your food will allow you to celebrate your meal and make it more satisfying. When you eat mindfully, you connect with the time and allow yourself a break from your day to enjoy yourself.

There is nothing more important than proper nutrition. We are given one vehicle – one body – that we use to travel around this physical globe. When it breaks down and stops working, we don't get to trade it in for a newer model. When the vehicle breaks down, our trip is over. Treat your body like a temple. And this starts by powering it with healthy, satisfying, nutrient-rich food that tastes great and is good for you.

Slow down and enjoy your food. You'll be glad you did.

Mindful listening

My wife likes to tell me I have selective hearing. In many ways, she's correct. My attention isn't always focused where it needs to be. This causes me to hear what is being said without focusing on what is being communicated. And despite what my wife thinks, this is actually a problem for both men and women – not just husbands.

Our ability to focus on what people say to us is greatly diminished when we are not mindfully listening to what is said to us. It's easy to become distracted by the outside and inside world, disengaging our attention with what people are saying to us.

I use mindful listening to not only help comprehend and remember what I'm told, but it has greatly improved my ability to communicate with others. Most people during a conversation are simply waiting for their turn to speak. They are not listening but rather waiting for an opening to say something. This is not a good way to communicate. How can you really understand what someone is saying if you are not listening but rather forming what you plan on saying in response?

When you talk, you hope people are actually listening to you. When you feel as if they are not, you tend to disengage with the conversation much quicker. When you learn to mindfully listen to someone, you connect with what they are saying. This level of focus attention on what the other person is saying can and will be felt by the people you speak with, and they often feel that they are better understood by you. One of the greatest compliments I can hope to receive is when someone says I am a good listener. It means I am mindfully listening to what they are saying. Nothing makes a person feel more valued than when they feel like they are being heard.

During my quiet meditation time, I will often simply listen to the sounds around me. I try to see how far away I can make out sounds, passing cars, birds chirping in the trees, a dog barking off in the distance. All of these sounds have the ability to connect us with the present moment. Being able to listen mindfully doesn't require another person to talk to you. The world has plenty to say to us. We simply need to practice how mindfully we listen.

Mindful seeing

As a creative person and an artist, the act of practicing mindful seeing is one of my most enjoyable activities and has had a positive impact on both my anxiety and my perspective on what's happening around me. There are two ways you can use mindful seeing to connect you with the present moment.

The first is taking time to simply slow down and look at the world around you. We take for granted so much of the beauty and wonder of what is around us every day. The colors, details, and textures, the depth and the richness of the items that surround us can be hypnotizing and awe-inspiring if we give them the space and the time to connect with us. As I sit here typing this chapter of my book, I am a guest at a wonderful bed and breakfast in northern New Hampshire. The weekend was a gift given to me from my wife so I could focus on my writing without distractions.

I am surrounded by so much color, so much light, and so many details in this antique home, I could get lost in them for hours. The desk I am sitting at is warm and rich with character and history. I look out the window, and I can see the branches of the tree gently swaying in the cool, crisp afternoon breeze. I study the curtains that adorn the window frame, gold and intricately stitched with a decorative design running down the length of the material, to where it softly touches the hardwood floors of the room.

Many of these items would normally go unnoticed by guests staying here. Often rushing through their day, hurrying to leave and take in the sights around this cozy little town. One could spend an entire day sightseeing and never leave this room. It is not our normal way to spend so much time on such little details. But I insist that it is within the details that you will find rest from your mind and your thoughts. Taking the time to focus on the details, getting lost in their splendor, is the shortest distance between anxiety and peace.

The other way in which we can use our sight to become more mindfully aware is to focus on the negative space between objects. If you are not familiar with the term "negative space," it is the area outside of an object, filling in the spaces and gaps of everything that is not part of the item. If you are looking at a chair, it is the space between the legs, the opening underneath the arms of the chair, and the space that surrounds and outlines the shape of the back. It is the space that is between you and everything else around you.

I've found this focus on the negative space to be incredibly helpful when I'm in crowded areas like supermarkets, shopping malls, or movie theaters, places that can cause those of us who struggle with anxiety to feel trapped and closed in. Often, I will shift my focus from the people filling the space to the area between each person, including above their heads. In really crowded places the open space above people can feel far more vast and empty than the space between each person near the floor. The people become a collection of shapes moving within a sea of emptiness, all connected and similar, yet all uniquely individual.

There is almost an out-of-body experience when you focus on the negative space around things rather than on the objects themselves. Walking down a hallway becomes a completely different experience when you are focusing on the space around you as you walk, feeling your body balance and move, the sensations of your feet striking the floor, the smells of the building you are in.

All of your senses combine to open your experience up in a way that you've never known before but one that has always been around you. You were always simply too busy and distracted by your thoughts to notice it.

This is how mindfulness impacts our lives: by taking us out of our heads and putting us back into the wonder of the world around us, a wonder that has always been there, patiently waiting for us to return.

"No one can make you feel inferior without your consent."
– Eleanor Roosevelt

CHAPTER 6: POSITIVE SELF-TALK

I sat hunched over in the small, uncomfortable wooden chair. It was in that moment the weight of my situation finally caught up with me.

"How are you doing?" she asked.

"Not good" was all I could muster before my voice cracked.

I'm not sure if it was the anger from fighting with my soon-to-be ex-wife, the sadness from being away from my kids, the realization that the woman I could finally see myself being happy with was moving across the country, or the exhaustion from working three jobs, but something inside of me just let go. I couldn't hold back. There was nothing I could do. I was lost and completely out of answers.

"What's going on?" she inquired again.

I couldn't speak. I just put my head between my hands and

began to cry.

"How did I end up here?" was all I could think to myself. Images from the past 35 years played back in my head. I struggled to make sense of it all. I had caused so much pain for so many people. I was creating the same scenario I swore I never would. I was divorcing my wife and putting my kids in the middle of a custody battle while simultaneously trying to put my life back together and be happy for the first time in a long time. I felt selfish. I felt like it was my fault. I felt like I had failed my family, my kids, and myself.

I love my kids more than anything in the world. And in truth, after my daughter Lili was born, my life changed dramatically, not just on the outside but on the inside as well. Lili wasn't a very good sleeper. At night, we would take turns sitting up with her, soothing her in the rocking chair or rubbing her back while she lay in her crib. I spent hours sitting in a dark, quiet room, holding my daughter and thinking. She was perfect to me. I couldn't imagine not always wanting to be there for her. Wanting to support and love her, always encouraging her to be anything she wanted to be and do anything she wanted to do. I wanted her to be happy. I wanted her to be brave and self-confident – to live life with wonder, passion and joy. I wanted her to be everything I wasn't and do everything I hadn't.

I saw myself as weak, lazy, irresponsible, and less than what I could have become. I always thought like I hadn't lived up to my potential. Worst of all, I believed my parents felt that way, too. I'd never had a very close relationship with either of them. Ever since I was young, I always felt that being close to one caused the other pain. My mother was extremely vocal about how she felt about my father. When I was around 10 years old, both of my parents remarried and started having more children. Soon they both had new babies and started making plans to move to make room for their expanding families. But I didn't want to move. I liked where I lived. I had friends in the neighborhood, and my best friend lived three houses down from me. We had a house on a lake where I spent all my time fishing and swimming. I was happy in that house. I was happy where we lived. Why did we have to move?

But there was no discussion. My mother's new husband wanted to build his own house. In his words, "This was her house, and it would never feel like it was mine." So we moved.

It was hard not to feel like I wasn't much of a priority anymore. Everything we did focused around my new little brother and stepfather. He wasn't a very affectionate man. He was quiet and intimidating. He worked construction and smoked, so he often smelled of cigarettes and freshly cut wood. I was an emotional kid who liked to draw and paint, and he didn't seem to have much use for me.

My own dad was a cop who hunted and also did construction. He also didn't show much interest in what I was into at the time. He often told me that I should get a job lettering trucks because someone he knew did that and made a lot of money. I didn't know anything about lettering trucks, nor did I have any interest in it. I wanted to paint pictures and shoot photos. He bought me a bow and arrow when I was a teenager. I think he thought he could take me hunting with him when I got older. We never went.

All of these thoughts, memories and images ran through my mind as I sat in that uncomfortable wooden chair, hands covering my face, eyes filled with tears. I knew why I was there. I was there because I would have wanted my daughter to have done what I did. I would have wanted my daughter to be happy and not live a life she didn't enjoy.

I had spent the past two years doing a mental exercise that had begun to shift how I looked at myself. Each time I felt anxious, afraid to try something, or unable to make a decision, I would imagine that it was my daughter coming to me with the exact same problem. I would picture us talking, and I would imagine giving her advice that I would hope she would follow. The interesting part was that the advice I would give to her was never the same advice

I would give to myself. It was easy for me to tell her what I thought she should do, but it never seemed to apply when I was on the receiving end of that same advice.

This made me wonder why the advice was good for her but not for me. Why did I believe what I said when I told her to do something, but I didn't believe it when I told it to myself?

I quickly came to a painful realization that it was because I didn't love myself the way I loved my daughter. It was easy for me to see her try and fail because I loved her so much, it didn't matter to me if she failed at something. She'd still always be perfect in my eyes.

After this, I started learning to love myself – or at least to give myself better advice. But a hard reality began to creep into my life. When I looked at my marriage and I thought about how I would advise my daughter if she were in my shoes, I came to a difficult conclusion. I realized that I would have told my daughter that if she wasn't happy, like I wasn't happy, that she needed to either fix the marriage or end it. And I had spent years trying to fix it already. Nothing had come from those efforts. I had no hope of anything ever really changing. I realized my marriage was over. It would still be another year before I built up the courage to act on that decision.

"You know why it's so hard for you to give yourself the same advice you give your daughter, right?" she asked in her thick, Hungarian accent.

The woman sitting across from me, listening to me tell my tale and sob uncontrollably in her office, was my therapist, Jutka. She was a smaller woman with strong hands, short gray hair, and a no B.S. attitude about her. She would sometimes swear during our sessions, other times she would just whisper the swear or spell it out. Before she said something inappropriate, she would state, "I probably shouldn't say this, but…" and then proceed to tell me to either get my shit together or that someone was being an ass. She had a way of cutting through my excuses and getting to the core of what I was dealing with. I had been seeing her as my therapist for the past month or so, and she reminded me a lot of my grandmother. I think that was why I was so comfortable with her.

"Look," she said, shifting in her seat as if she were going to lean in and share a secret. "When you talk to your daughter in your head, the voice that you hear giving her advice is the voice of her father talking to her."

I nodded, wondering where she was going with this.

"But when you talk to yourself, the voice you are hearing giving you advice is not yours but the voice of your mother and father talking to you."

I paused for a moment and let that sink in. It was painful and eye opening all at the same time. Like usual, she was right. I hadn't really thought of it that way. I always looked at it as if I didn't love myself enough, but the reason I didn't love myself is because my self-worth came from how I was treated by my parents. If they made me feel unloved and unwanted, that was how I was inevitably going to treat myself. And I had.

"You are right," I said, wiping the remaining tears from my red, swollen eyes.

"So what you need to do now is learn to parent yourself the way you parent your daughter."

It became clear to me in a way that it hadn't been before. I had already begun doing this for a while but I had never put it into that context before. I didn't have the parents I wanted to have. I know they did their best, but they made a lot of mistakes. Their mistakes left me feeling worthless and broken. I believed I deserved the way they treated me. It was as if I had done something that caused them to treat me the way that they did. In reality, they treated me the way they had been treated as children, probably by parents who themselves had also been treated the same way by their parents.

Our parents are our first real teachers in life. They set the bar for how high we hold our self-esteem, how we see ourselves, and what we will tolerate from how the world treats us.

I wasn't going to make the same mistakes my parents made with me. I wasn't going to put my children into the same situation my parents put me in. They may end up being from a divorced family, but that didn't mean they were going to suffer.

I realized what I needed to do. I had to forgive myself for how I had been treating myself. I needed to make sure I stayed true to how I wanted to treat and raise my children, with as much love, support, and respect as I could. And I was also going to become a parent to myself and work on healing those wounds that had been there for so long. It was going to take some work and reprogramming of how I responded to myself, but I knew I had to do this for myself and for my kids.

I left Jutka's office that day with a new understanding of who I was and who I was about to become. My kids were going to have a great childhood, not because I was perfect but because I would not let a day go by where they didn't know they were loved and supported. I'd always be there for my kids, and now I'd always be there for myself. I'd fall back in love with who I was, I'd forgive myself for my mistakes, and I'd begin to build the life I had always dreamed I'd have. I was now building my life from a place of love rather than a place of fear.

The journey I went through is very similar to a lot of people's journeys when they build a life out of fear. We learn to make decisions based on trying to control an outcome. Instead, we should be creating what we want to have happen and we should do it from a place of love. But before I could do that, I had to become aware of the depths of my issues and learn to hear the way I spoke to myself with clear, mindful listening.

There is only one person that is with you from the moment you are born until the day you die. This person is the most important person to your success. No matter who else comes into your life, if you are not on good speaking terms with this person, it will have a negative impact on everything you do or consider doing. This person is your coach, your cheerleader and your biggest supporter, and this person also is responsible for lifting you up or keeping you down. How far you go in life is completely dependent upon your relationship with this person.

This person is you.

I had no idea how mean I had become to myself. As far back as I can remember, I spoke to myself in a negative, degrading, disrespectful, and unkind manner. I spent all my life telling myself I couldn't do things when I should have been telling myself I could. What was even worse was the fact that my tone and hurtful speech had become such a habit that I was completely unaware that it was taking place.

My default setting in life was one of negativity, fear, anger, and a general sense of "what I don't want." That is what creating from fear is like.

At our core, we are all creators. We all have a passion for expanding our lives and building something that impacts our legacy. Everything we build is the manifestation of that energetic pull toward our creative desires. Creation can be a long process that requires discipline, order, passion, drive, commitment, patience, and love. We as a society have lost much of that drive to be the creators in our lives. We've become brainwashed into the idea that we are simply consumers of things that have been created by others. We doubt our skills and our abilities, and we are taught that striving for more than we have is the negative trait of those who are selfish and gluttonous. That somehow wanting to create something that is lasting and impactful means you must hurt other people in the process.

This is creating from a place of fear. Creating a business that requires you to crush your competition rather than celebrating their achievements along with your own is not creation from a loving place. We push ourselves to be better than everyone else rather than seeing everyone as the same as ourselves. We compete rather than support. And then we internalize that method inward and treat ourselves like our own worst enemy.

We are raised as children to believe the world is a cold, dark place that we have to be prepared to manage. That no one gives you anything and you have to earn and fight for everything you get. No one is going to hand it to you. You have to go out there and take it. This creates a fearful mentality. Instead of seeing others as people we live with and as a community, we look with suspicious eyes at our fellow men, fearing they will take what we have if we do not take what they have first.

All this pressure and negativity eats away at the very fiber of our being. We did not come to this earth to take but to experience. We are not here to win but to play. There is nothing to win. We do not take anything with us when we go. All we can do is leave behind something greater than ourselves. Our legacy is how the world remembers our impact. And that legacy begins not when our lives end but when they start. Each action we take, how we speak to each other, and how we choose to impact those we come into contact with, those are the materials from which our legacy is built.

But we must also understand that our world is simply a reflection of ourselves. Because our perspective shapes our reality, when we hold hate or fear in our hearts, that is what we present to the world and what the world presents back to us. This is the biggest challenge in our ability to create the life we want: We give our power away believing that the world changes us. In truth, we change the world. We do this based on what we empower the world to become. We are the masses. We are the creators. We dictate what is and is not acceptable in our lives.

The hate that exists in the world is a product of fear. Men and women who fear others must overcome it through control and domination. They take rather than give, and they fight rather than love. We've created a cycle where you are either dominant or dominated. We then see ourselves in these terms. We are either strong or weak, we are brave or cowards, we are winners or losers.

Such hard-edged, black-and-white options are not realistic to how our lives really work. We are all things at all times. We are infinite potential at all moments. We are both winners and losers.

Sometimes we win and sometimes we do not: This does not mean that we should forever be judged as one or the other. It is this limiting belief that causes us to pick one side and decide that is how we will identify ourselves for the rest of our lives. We look at ourselves in the mirror and either we see a winner or a loser, a leader or a follower, someone who is strong or someone who is weak. How you see yourself is a reflection of how you believe the world sees you. But in truth, the world only sees you in this manner because it is the face you've decided to show the world. It doesn't have to be that way.

Henry Ford, the automobile manufacturer, once said, "If you think you can do a thing or think you can't do a thing, you're right." How we see ourselves, the picture we have of who we are and what we are capable of, is what creates the world around us.

People spend most of their lives looking at what has happened to them and around them, and they say, "I'm the way I am because of my circumstances." What they should be saying is, "I have experienced a lot of things. What can I learn from them?"

Unfortunately, we become programmed by the things in our lives and falsely believe they are permanently our identity rather than just a bump in the road of our lives. We get stuck in a pattern of limiting beliefs and fearful assumptions, and we stop creating. We lose our spiritual and emotional value for all that we can accomplish, and we settle on a life we think the world is willing to give us. We stop believing in our own greatness because we compare ourselves to others in a way that doesn't inspire us to greatness – rather, it intimidates us into submission.

I was one of these people. I had let my life convince me I was not worthy of great things. I had believed the things I was told and locked myself into a story I believed to be true and permanent.

The facts of my life were just the details of its moments, not my definition. I let those facts limit the person I thought I could become and I believe it was life doing that to me. Life does not limit what you can become; only you can do that.

I have spent the better part of the past few years focusing on changing the way I see myself, speak to myself, and feel about myself. The picture of who I was on the inside needed to change before the picture of who I was on the outside ever would. This is simply the way it is. If you want to change your outer world, start by changing your inner one.

To quote Mahatma Gandhi, "We but mirror the world. All the tendencies present in the outer world are to be found in the world of our body. If we could change ourselves, the tendencies in the world would also change. As a man changes his own nature, so does the attitude of the world change towards him. This is the divine mystery supreme. A wonderful thing it is and the source of our happiness. We need not wait to see what others do."

Or, as many have simplified this to mean, "Be the change you want to see in the world."

This means that we must first change our inner view of who we are before the outer world will see us that way. By changing how we feel about ourselves on the inside, it changes how we walk, how we talk, how we carry ourselves, the way we move through our day, the amount of confidence we have, and what we will and will not allow regarding treatment from other people. It doesn't mean you have to become snobby, rude, or unfeeling toward other people. This is the attitude society will place on people with confidence and who feel secure in who they are. Most people lack these skills so they diminish their importance or vilify those people who demonstrate such qualities. Being confident is not the same as being cocky. It also doesn't mean everything always works out exactly the way we thought they would. Having confidence simply means that you have a belief in your own ability to get something done, no matter how many times you need to try.

Confident people fail. Everyone fails. But people who possess a positive mind-set and a confident demeanor understand that failure is part of success. Failure doesn't define who you are. You do not become a failure; you simply experience failure just like you experience everything else in your life. You can experience seeing a beautiful sunrise in the morning, but that doesn't mean you become a beautiful sunrise.

We need to learn to break the habit of categorizing and labeling ourselves and others based on the activities they participate in regularly. It isn't bad, but it can be limiting to our potential. Because you are a parent, it doesn't mean you can't be a businessperson or an artist or writer also. It simply means you do many things. While you are in the moment of watching your children, you are acting as a parent. When you are writing, you are acting as a writer. When you are at your office, you are running your business. We use these labels to help communicate with others about the activities we do with more frequency, but we shouldn't limit what we can do by what we do most often.

Now, based on the idea that through repetition we develop skills and eventually mastery of certain activities, we often connect our identity much more closely with some activities over others. But if we choose to identify as something in particular, we should be careful as to how closely we identify with this action or activity. Often people who too closely identify with one aspect of their lives have a difficult time dealing with their identity when that activity is taken away.

Professional athletes go through this after they retire. They spend so many years playing a sport that they love, oftentimes starting when they are just children. They become identified by the sport they play, but when their career ends, either due to retirement or injury, they often struggle to figure out whom they are.

Celebrities also go through this when they fear their looks or popularity are beginning to fade. This is why we see so many celebrities having plastic surgery, hoping to hang on to their youthful self. They identify as being the young, beautiful actor or actress, but as they age, they struggle to hang on to that identity.

This is something everyone experiences on some level. You don't have to be a professional athlete or a movie star to feel like you're losing who you use to be. As we age, our bodies change. If we identify too closely to a temporary version of our self, we will struggle as that version transforms into a new and different version. The goal is to learn to be happy with the person we are and build a life we find fulfilling. But how can we build that fulfilling life if we have no idea what makes us feel fulfilled?

We often head down a path in life that we think will make us happy. Many people either go to college for something they think they want to do as a career that they will enjoy – or, at minimum, pay the bills. Others learn a trade and go to work using their hands and hard work to pay bills and support themselves and their families. Still other people simply float through life without a real sense of direction or purpose. They wait for something to come along that looks interesting and they say, "I'll give that a shot!" Then years later, they try to figure out how they ended up where they are and what they can do to change it.

We hear people say things like "happiness is an inside job" or "you can't love someone else if you don't love yourself," but what do those things really mean? And how can you apply these things to your everyday life so that they have impact?

I'm going to share with you the actual steps I used to learn to change how I spoke to myself and how I learned to turn my life around from the inside out. It's important that you understand that these are not just ideas to think about and say, "Yes, that makes sense" and then just return to your everyday way of life. I want you to actually put these steps into practice in your life.

I've said this a few times in this book and I hope that it is beginning to sink in at this point, but I'll say it again just to drive the point home: If you don't take action in your life to change things, nothing is going to ever change! By reading this book, you'll make me happy, but not as happy as if you put these steps into practice and improve the quality and happiness of your life. That is my goal, and it should be your goal, too.

Keep a Negative Thoughts List

Most people would say that they are probably too hard on themselves or that they could be a bit nicer in the way they speak to themselves. Having an idea of the way you talk to yourself – and actually seeing what and how often you say negative things to yourself – can be an eye-opening experience. It's similar to tracking the amount of calories you eat in a day. We all assume we probably eat too much, but if you've ever gone through the trouble of actually logging what you eat and calculating your calories, you'd probably be amazed at how many added calories you are consuming in a single day.

I spent last years working on my diet in much the same way I had been working on my mental health. I used a smartphone app called Cronometer, and I scanned and logged everything I ate for six months. What I learned was that it was extremely easy to eat for more junk when you are not paying attention to what you are eating. But as soon as I had to start tracking what I ate, I become far more aware of what I was consuming and it changed my habits quickly.

Unfortunately, there is no Negative Thinking app for you to download and use, so you'll have to use an old-fashioned notebook and pen. I would recommend that you do not use your smartphone or digital device for this or any other writing assignments listed in this book. The reason is that these devices can be incredibly distracting. Most of us receive emails, text messages, social media notifications, and the occasional phone call on our smartphones. So any time you can use pen and paper, I highly recommend you do so. It also helps to engage different parts of your brain that need the exercise as well.

The idea is to spend time over a few days or even weeks and write down every negative thought you have about yourself each time you have one. No matter how small or trivial it might seem, if you have a thought about yourself, write it down. If you are not sure if it's negative, write it down anyway and you can sort it out later.

Some common thoughts you may find you have are:
I don't look good in that.
I feel or look fat.
I can't do this.
I hope I don't mess this up.
I don't want to go to work today.
I hate Mondays.
My life sucks.
I need a better job.
Who would ever hire me?
I'm too old to do that.
I need a better life.
I'm always late.
Why can't I be better at that?
What if I make a mistake?
What if they don't like me?
I'll never be able to remember all this.
I probably can't do it.
I'm just not very good at that.
I can never think of any good ideas.
Why can't I be that creative?
My house is always a mess.

Does any of this sound familiar? Now, you may be thinking some of these are just observations. It's not that you are being negative, but you are just stating a fact. Maybe your house is a mess, and maybe you are always late. But what ends up happening is that each time we point out something we see as a flaw or something we don't like about our lives, we are actually beating ourselves up over their existence. There is a big difference between when we say, "I have to take out the trash" versus "My house looks like a dump." One of these is a chore that needs to be taken care of and the other is a negative comment. When we make negative comments, we are subtly blaming ourselves for the fact that we didn't clean the house or we didn't show up on time for an event.

Now, I have some bad news, good news, and great news regarding some of these revelations. The bad news is, yes, some of these are absolutely your fault. This isn't about not taking responsibility for your life. Your life is the way it is because of the choices you've made and others you've decided to accept.

The good news is that once you learn to take responsibility for these things, you'll realize that you can also fix them, make them better, or remove them all together. By utilizing some of the tools in this book, such as mindful living and practicing with intention, you can learn to recognize, address, and change these types of behaviors and actions to help dramatically improve your life.

And the great news is that we are not interested in fixing these things right now. We only want to start listing these negative comments for two important reasons.

Reason number one is that you need to see exactly how hard you are being on yourself. You need to wake yourself up and open your eyes to the type of hurtful, destructive, and counterproductive language you use to try and "motivate" yourself to be a better person. The truth is you are already an amazing person! You're just so busy beating yourself up over every little thing you do, you've lost sight of all the things you do well and all of the strengths you have.

Reason number two is so that we can start to take these negative comments and find replacement thoughts for you to start using in their place.

Positive Replacement Thoughts

After you've spent a few days or so going through the process of writing down all your negative comments, take a little bit of time to look for common themes or repetitive comments that you can group together. They may be something about your appearance, work performance, or personal traits such as being lazy, stupid, unworthy, or unlovable. See if you can find the things you seem to say to yourself the most often, with the most passion or believe with the most conviction.

Take a clean sheet of paper and create two columns. Write "negative" over one column and "positive" over the other. Take each of your negative thoughts that repeat the most in your life, and write them down under your negative thoughts column. Then next to each negative, under the positive column, I want you to come up with a positive thought you can replace your negative one with.

If you are not sure, here are some examples:

Negative:	**Positive:**
I can't do this.	I can do this.
This will never work.	This is going to be amazing.
I'm too weak.	I'm getting stronger every day.
Who would ever love me?	I'm a beautiful person who deserves love.
What if I fail?	I am going to either succeed or learn and improve.
I'm stupid.	I am open to learning new things every day.
I'm going to freak out.	I am going to be okay.
I'm so scared.	I feel excited by something new, and I welcome this challenge.

This may seem a little too positive for some people, especially those who have been suffering from anxiety for a long time. We convince ourselves that we can't do things to such a degree that we believe our limitations are facts rather than opinions. Your negative thoughts are simply opinions – and they can be changed. But you need to develop the habit of looking for the positive language rather than the negative language.

And if you still think this is too fake and over the top with positivity, please recognize that you have already been too fake and over the top with negativity. You've already been using this technique for years, just in a very destructive and self-deprecating way. And how is that working out for you?

Think about how anxious you feel every day. Think about how difficult it is to build the courage to try new things, to push yourself past your limits or to have the trust in yourself that you can accomplish your goal or that you even deserve to accomplish your goals. You feel this way because you've used your negative thinking to reinforce this belief system inside yourself. All you are doing now is taking that exact pattern and adjusting it from a negative habit to a positive one. I'm not asking you to change the action you are taking, just adjusting it from negative to positive. You will still be talking to yourself using your thoughts. You'll just be doing it with love instead of hate, and you'll be supporting yourself rather than discouraging yourself.

This action is the beginning of changing the image you hold in your mind of who you are. It is the cornerstone of all the work you'll do moving forward. When you learn to see a clear, positive, and loving picture of the person you are, you will let go of some of the damaging and incorrect images you've been carrying around in your mind for years. Images that have been put there by other people, by incorrect beliefs, by negative experiences you've incorrectly blamed yourself for and by patterns of negativity you have inflicted on your self image for years.

To this day, I still practice replacing my negative thoughts with positive ones. If you learn to do one thing from this book, make it this one!

Fabulous Five-Year Plan

This part is for a little ways after you've been doing some work on improving yourself and repairing your self-image, but it is a key component to creating a new life. It is finding the answer to the question we always wonder about but never take the time to answer.

Where are you heading in life?

We often associate this type of question with something people ask during job interviews or performance reviews. It's the old "where do you see yourself in five years?" question that is meant to figure out if you are the right long-term fit for a company or for a certain position. But it is a far more important indicator for what you want to create and if you are going to create it.

Let's start with the obvious point that most people have never bothered to sit and figure out what they wanted to create in their lives over the next five years. We make grocery lists, to-do lists for our daily chores, and even pro and con lists for decisions we have to make. But how many of you have ever sat down and actually written out what your goals and dreams are? How many of you have taken the time to think about what your life would look like if you could create the perfect life for yourself. Who would be in it? Where would you live? What would you be doing? What would you look like?

These are some of the key questions we should focus on in order to put a plan together to build our future. But what I have found is that instead of focusing on what we want, most people focus on what they don't want! They don't want to be broke. They don't want a dead-end job. They don't want to be alone. They don't want to be unhappy.

Placing attention on the things you don't want simply keeps your focus on those things. We need to learn to shift our focus, much like we do with our thoughts about ourselves, from the negative to the positive. We need to have a clear vision of what we want to create and then start to take action to support that vision.

Like I said before, this is a more advanced exercise that could be talked about at much greater length than I am going to here. I just want to introduce the idea for anyone ready to go past overcoming anxiety and fear and really take control to build his or her dream life.

Essentially, what you do is take a piece of paper and pen and write out in detail everything you would create for yourself over the next five years if you knew no matter what you attempted you would not fail. Not necessarily that you wouldn't still be fearful of doing it, but that if you did it, you wouldn't fail.

And to make it a little easier to organize, I broke my own personal identity plan up into three main parts: personality traits, physical and health traits, and overall goals.

The key to doing this exercise properly is to make sure you write everything down as if it has already happened.

Here's an example. Instead of writing "I hope to be running a small business online," write "I am the proud owner of a successful online business selling my hand-made notecards to people all over the world." Don't say, "I want to be able to speak to people without feeling nervous," but rather "I feel comfortable and relaxed when speaking to people for the first time and I make new friends easily and often."

Write down as much detail as you can as they specifically relate to all the things you would do, create, and/or have if failure was not an option. Don't worry about being too realistic or too crazy with what you write, just try to be honest about what it is you'd like to establish for your over in the next five years.

Once you have this document written, keep it with you and read it at least once a once a week or even once a day. Personally, I read mine once in the morning and once before bed. It keeps me focused on what I want to create for myself, keeps me clear on the type of person I want to be and it helps me reinforce the positive self-talk I want to use in order to rebuild my confidence and support my life goals. The key to writing it as if you already have these things is that, when you read them over and over again, stating them as facts that have already happened, this will begin to train your brain to see them as part of your everyday reality rather than always being something for the future. It will help reprogram your mind to build the life you want as if it is not only possible but already a reality.

And the final and most important part of this process is that you need to take action. Telling yourself that these things are part of who you already are is an important step in the reprogramming part of dealing with our anxiety and negative self-image. But wishing and dreaming alone isn't going to get you any closer to your goals, your dreams, and your new life if you do not put the right action into place to make them a reality.

When you see yourself as this new person, you need to begin to act like it. The process of making these statements to yourself weekly or daily will build the confidence and the positive expectations that will allow you to start taking the necessary steps to put action behind the emotion. This is the difference between thinking positive and being positive. Just thinking about the things you want is only half the battle. For anxiety sufferers and people trapped in the repetitive loop of self-doubt, it's an extremely large part of that battle, but it's still not enough to really create that change you are looking for.

When you see yourself as the person who is confident, you need to begin to take action like someone who is confident. When confronted with a situation that you would have normally backed away from in the past because your mind would have jumped in and said, "you can't do that," your new mind will think, "I am a confident person who can do that." And then you actually do it.

And the more you do the action that supports this new image you have of yourself, the more you solidify the reality: This is now who you are. You will then begin to retrain your brain to respond to these situations with your new mind-set rather than your old one.

So the first step is to see it, then to speak it, and, finally, act it into reality. If you follow these steps, there is nothing you won't be able to accomplish.

Create Your Positivity Vision Board

If you've never heard of a vision board, there is probably a good chance that you are either very new to the self-help arena or you've been living under a rock for the past few decades. Either way let me give you a 10,000-foot view of what vision boards are and why I love them so much.

A vision board, or dream board as some call them, is a collage of meaningful, inspirational, and emotion-evoking images that represent all the things you want to create, experience, build, explore, and attract into your life. It is very similar to writing out your five-year plan, but it focuses on using images rather than words to create the emotional connection between what it feels like to have these things and actually having them in your life.

The universe communicates through the feelings of emotion. The more you can create the emotional feeling within yourself, the more easily aligned you will become with those things in your physical life.

Most people approach things saying, "Once I have this or that, I will feel happy." But in truth, being able to feel that emotion before you actually have these things makes it far easier to create and achieve them, because in your mind you already have these things and are living that life. This causes you to act in the way that is normally accustomed to someone already living that life. And as you take action like that person, you realize that you've already become that person.

Now, does this mean you should walk into a car dealership and write a check for the most expensive sports car on the lot, even though you only have a few hundred dollars in your account? Absolutely not. But you should start to imagine yourself having that car and acting as if you are well on your way to owning it. This will cause you to make choices and take action in your life that will put you on the path to making owning that car a reality.

But a vision board is a lot more than just putting up pictures of fancy cars, exotic locations, and piles of money. It's about looking deep inside to discover how you want to feel about yourself, and then using visually stimulating images that invoke those feelings you want to feel. Most people want to drive a sports car because at some point in their life, they were taught that if they had a sports car, they would be highly respected or looked up to. Now, owning a sports car may not actually make this true, but the important part is the feeling they are trying to attain rather than the actual car. There are other ways of creating that feeling inside yourself that don't require you to purchase anything. But unless you learn to be self-aware enough to recognize the emotional desire behind the object or the accomplishment, you can't begin to fill that void in the right way.

You'll end up doing what most people do when they reach a level of success that allows them to simply purchase a sports car. They feel happy for a little while and then end up purchasing another sports car because the feeling disappears shortly after the first car is home. Using your vision board to try and collect "stuff" is the wrong way to use it. It isn't about the luxury items but about the feelings that make you want them.

So if you can fill your vision board with things that create that feeling inside you, it will help align your actions with those feelings. When your feelings and actions are in alignment, you are in what most people refer to as the "zone" or the "flow." That is the sweet spot where you can begin to build, create, and succeed at things with ease and enjoyment. It's when everything seems to be moving in the right direction in an almost effortless fashion.

That is why I like to suggest people do the five-year plan and the vision board exercise together, because they will both help reinforce creating the feelings first, allowing you to take better action to build the life that will truly make you happy rather than just chasing dreams you think will make you happy.

Again, this is just an overview of putting together a vision board and why I like to use it, so I will not go into any great detail. There are some amazing programs out there that can teach you how to build your specific vision board. There are also many great free resources you can find if you search for vision boards online.

For me, I simply broke up my board into categories that were important to me at that time in my life.

Some examples of categories are:
- Money
- Travel/Pleasure
- Relationships/Family
- Career
- Health
- Education
- Creative
- Personality Traits

Once you've picked the categories you want your board to focus on, it's time to find your images. They can be images of anything as long as they invoke the emotions attached to what you are trying to create. It doesn't have to make sense to anyone else as long as it makes sense to you.

Here's an example from my board. I have a photo of Bruce Lee, the famous martial artist and actor. Growing up, I loved karate movies and no one was better in my opinion than Lee. He was dedicated and committed to being the world's best martial artist, and it showed in his work ethic. He trained at a level that most people would never be able to commit to. He mastered his own body and pushed past his limits, which made him one of the most feared and revered fighters in the world. Lee not only mastered many different styles of martial arts, he also developed his own unique style and philosophy of fighting, which he called jeet kune do. He then traveled the world teaching and sharing what he knew with others. When I look at his picture, without having to put anything into words, it creates a sense of commitment, discipline, intelligence, and physical excellence that touches on many aspects I want to incorporate into my life. Someone might see his picture on my vision board and ask, "You want to be Bruce Lee?"

It isn't about wanting to be him, rather it's about embodying what his image symbolizes to me, of always pushing and striving to be the best both mentally and physically through hard work, commitment, focus, and passion. I feel those things when I look at his picture, so his picture is on my board.

Keep this in mind when you look for pictures for your board. If a picture of a mansion creates the feeling of abundance in you, put it up there. But be careful not to put pictures up that you think you are supposed to. If you feel a sense of guilt or selfishness about putting a picture of a mansion on your board, that is the emotion you will feel when you look at it. This will simply work to reinforce the negative emotions we are trying to move away from. Maybe someday, once you've dug deep and done your shadow work to understand why you associate a mansion with feeling guilty or selfish, maybe then you can use that picture. But if you are not there now, don't use it. Find something else that creates the feelings you want to generate and use those images.

Once you've completed your board, make sure you put it someplace where you will see it every day. Hang it up in your office, put it in your bedroom, stick it to your refrigerator, or hang it in your living room. Just put it someplace where you will look at it and feel those emotions.

And make some time each day to sit, relax, and focus on the feelings that arise when looking at your board. It isn't just about seeing it and running past like it's any other picture you have on your walls. It's about mindfully focusing your attention on those feelings and allowing them to permeate your inner self in a deep and meaningful way.

Be mindful in how you take in the images and feelings from your vision board. Make sure you treat yourself to time to dream and welcome the feelings you want to have more of in your life. Like meditation, mindfulness, and any other practice talked about in this book, if you do not put them into action and find time to practice them every day, they will not be able to help you in the way they are capable of. Make this action a priority in your life, and you will see how your priorities will change.

"If you knew what I know about the power of giving, you would not let a single meal pass without sharing it in some way."
– Buddha

CHAPTER 7: GIVE TO RECEIVE

We all have the ability to pull ourselves out of a funk. There are many ways to do this, but one of the most effective is to focus not on ourselves but on others.

No matter how shitty my day is going, an act of kindness toward another person never fails to lift my spirits, make me smile, and shift my mind-set from negative to positive.

It doesn't have to be a large act; you don't have to buy someone a car or make a mortgage payment for him or her that month. Just a small act of kindness can quickly lift your spirits, readjust your perspective, and make you feel good inside.

Doing nice things for others is such a simple gesture, but it's often one we overlook in society today. Our lives are so hectic and fast paced, we can lose sight of the other people around us. We see them as competition or obstacles we need to navigate around in order to get where we need to be. We see other people as those who can take away our happiness or cause us to suffer, so we avoid connecting with them to protect ourselves.

When we do want to help other people, we often find ourselves questioning how much they'll appreciate what we do. We question if they are deserving of our kindness by placing an expectation on what they'll do or how they should respond to our generosity or kindness.

Have you ever seen a homeless person on the street and questioned what he would do with the money you gave him? I know many people who refuse to help homeless people because they believe one of the following statements:

"They will just spend the money on booze or drugs."

"They need to get a job and earn their money like I do."

"They are just scamming the system and probably don't really need it."

"They got themselves into this situation, so they can get themselves out."

Or even worse, have you become blind to the homeless people in your area entirely? Have they become such a common sight to you that you don't see them as people who are suffering and living on the street? They've simply become visual elements of your surroundings, like potholes, puddles, or dog shit on the sidewalk. You only see them with enough attention to avoid making contact so they don't negatively impact you and your ability to safely get where you need to go.

But homeless people are an extreme example of those in need. What about other people in need who are less obvious? A mother trying to keep two children in check while carrying bags and struggling to open a door? A man lost in his thoughts trying to pay for his coffee and make it to work on time? Or the cashier working at a store trying to make a living the best way she can?

We all struggle in some way. Sometimes those struggles seem small compared to those of others, but our struggles are our own. They impact our lives and, in the moment, can seem just as daunting and insurmountable as any other problem facing other people.

When we become more aware of what is around us, we'll begin to see that there is no shortage of people who could use a hand, a smile, or a kind gesture. We have the ability to make a positive impact on people each day, and, in doing so, we also make a positive impact on our own life.

The feeling of helping another person is so unique and powerful, it's often hard to explain to others. There is a sense of connecting with another person, a feeling of love and happiness that warms you from the inside. It's incredible how such a large feeling can be generated by a small act. But it can happen at any time and be shared between anyone.

When you hold a door open for someone, and she looks at you and smiles, there is a connection that is made, if only for a brief moment, that makes you feel part of something larger. It's a moment that transcends labels, religion, social standing, race, or political beliefs.

It simply becomes about one human being helping another, and it is powerful.

I first experienced the transformational power of helping others during my youth, playing high school football. It feels a bit cliché telling old football stories. I feel a bit like Al Bundy from the 1990's television show *Married with Children* bragging about the four touchdowns he scored in a single game for Polk High School. And while this story does focus around my years playing high school football, I assure you this is not one of those stories.

I was a very active child. I loved playing with my friends outside, running around in the woods near my house, swimming in the lake where I grew up, and riding my bike around our neighborhood. I also enjoyed sports. I played soccer, baseball, and basketball at different times throughout my youth.

Unfortunately, due to my anxiety, I didn't stick with any sport for too long. Eventually, something would happen that caused me to get nervous or worry that I wasn't very good. Instead of sticking with it and practicing so I could get better, I would instead become consumed with my inability to do it and eventually I would get discouraged and quit.

So when I announced to my mother that I wanted to play football, she was not overly supportive. She had seen me start and stop so many things growing up, I'm sure she saw it as just one more activity I would quit when things got hard. She also worried for my safety. Football is a very physical sport and injuries are common. With all the information we have today regarding concussions and traumatic brain injury issues related to contact sports, looking back I can see that her concerns were obviously valid.

She tried to discourage me from going out for the team.

"You don't know how to play football," she said.

"I'll learn," I replied.

"It's very dangerous. What if you get hurt? You're not really tough enough to play football."

"I won't get hurt. The school gives us equipment to wear. I'll be fine."

"Okay," she finally said. "But if you get hurt, I don't want to hear about it."

At the time, her dismissal of my wanting to play felt very much like rejection. As a parent, I can appreciate her not wanting me to get hurt. But as a child, the way she went about trying to discourage me had a lasting impact on my confidence. In spite of her warnings and lack of support, I decided I would go out for the team.

I didn't know much about football. No one in my family ever played, and we didn't watch it much in our house. My mother didn't watch sports. My dad was always working, so he didn't spend much time in front of the television, and my grandparents were big baseball fans.

In truth, I wanted to play because that's what everyone else was going to do. The year before, my family had moved to a new town. I didn't know anyone, so in order to try and fit in, I became a follower. I didn't know my way around the social circles in my new school, but I had somehow lucked into becoming friendly with the most popular kid in my grade. His name was Rich, and he was cool. I quickly went from being known as the "new kid" to being known as "Rich's friend." It felt like a step in the right direction. So, when Rich decided the summer before our freshman year that he was going to play football, that meant I was going to play, too.

Uxbridge, Massachusetts, was a very small town. We had ten players going out for the freshman football team that year. And if you don't know anything about football, it takes eleven players to field a team. In other words, as long as you had a pulse and a willingness to get hit, you were going to play.

They added two sophomores so we could have eleven players and one substitute, in case someone got hurt. We were all pretty bad at first, but we had a lot of fun and eventually got better. Our coach, Mr. Donatelli, was also the high school gym teacher. He was an older, gruff man who would yell when he talked and often followed up what he said with an enthusiastic blow to our helmets with his clipboard. It didn't hurt, but the sound of the board reverberating off the plastic helmet would echo in our ears, making it a very unpleasant experience.

We got hazed by the seniors, used as tackling dummies for the varsity team during practice, and we were given the oldest, smelliest equipment the school had to offer. But we were a team, and I became hooked.

I played in ten games my freshman year. My parents didn't come to a single one.

My sophomore year, I went out for the team again. Now we were playing on the junior varsity team, mostly made up of sophomores and one or two juniors who weren't good enough to play full time on the varsity team. Some of us even got some playing time on the varsity team, including me. I logged enough minutes in varsity games that I earned a varsity letter for football. Being a sophomore with a varsity letter was a pretty big deal at the time. I finally felt like I was getting good at something, and I liked it.

I played in twelve junior varsity and twelve varsity games that year. Again, my parents didn't come to a single game.

The start of my junior year was hard for me. My anxiety had gotten really bad. I hated school, and I didn't have many close friends. I had started drinking once I got into high school. When you're a follower, that's what you do. I got in trouble a couple of times, and I was banned from hanging out with Rich and all my other friends. I worked at the local supermarket so I could make enough money to buy a car, and I played football. Other than that, I felt isolated and alone.

So when the football season started, I had high expectations. I assumed I'd be a starter on the varsity team since I had already played well my sophomore year. If not a starter, I at least expected to get a lot of playing time. Playing football seemed to be the only thing that brought me any joy, and I was going to make the most of it.

But as the season started, I found myself quickly relegated to the second- and third-string teams, often playing with the younger, less talented players. We played a couple of practice games, and I got almost no playing time with the varsity team. All my friends were playing, and I was standing on the sidelines with the freshmen and sophomore players, just watching. When it came time to list the starters for the varsity team, my name was nowhere to be found. And then things went from bad to worse.

Varsity players were not allowed to play with the junior varsity team. JV games didn't count in the standings, and the coach didn't want to risk a varsity player getting hurt, so all players deemed important were banned from playing.

Only three juniors were asked to dress for the junior varsity games. I was one of them. I was crushed! I felt like I had basically been told, "We don't care if you get hurt because we don't need you." All my friends were starters, and I was a scrub.

I was completely embarrassed. I came to the conclusion that I must not have been as good as I thought I was for the coach to have relegated me to the JV team. The entire school would know I was playing with the underclassmen while everyone else was playing in the games that really mattered.

I wanted to quit. Why should I subject myself to this type of humiliation? I had to dress and travel to games on Thursday afternoons while all my friends were getting ready to play under the lights on Friday nights. Not to mention this was my third year playing, and still not a single person from my family had ever come to see me play. I wondered, "What was the point?"

There was only one reason for me not to quit. I loved to play. When I was on the field running around, calling plays, and making tackles, I felt alive. Everything else in my life seemed to disappear. I loved being out there, even if everyone else thought I wasn't very good. I didn't want to quit because I wanted to play. The joy I felt on the field outweighed the embarrassment I felt off the field.

So I kept playing. Each week, while my friends were going over plays for the weekend's big game, I was on a bus with the younger kids, driving to some dirt patch in the middle of nowhere, playing in games no one cared about but us.

And I had so much fun!

Because I was one of the oldest players on the team, I began feeling not just like a player, but a coach. I enjoyed helping the younger kids understand the plays and how to improve their technique. I encouraged them to keep trying and to keep working. During practice, when all the players were together, I focused on the younger players, making sure they didn't get discouraged if they got beat by a better, older player. I found myself wanting to set a good example for the younger players, so I pushed myself harder so they would push themselves harder.

Our coach had strict rules about off-the-field conduct. If players got in trouble at school, showed up late for practice, or weren't conducting themselves properly during practice, they had to run extra conditioning after practice was over. Oftentimes, I would run alongside these players, encouraging them to keep going.

I would be just as exhausted as they were, but for some reason, I got this extra boost of energy when I helped them. When they saw me running with them, pushing them to keep going, they usually responded by pushing themselves harder. And when they did, I felt a sense of pride for them. It was as if I had been lifted up through what they had accomplished. That feeling made the physical pain of all the extra running disappear, and I felt amazing.

In a year where all my expectations seemed to have not been met, I focused on my actions and what I could control, and it turned out to be more rewarding than I could ever have expected.

Little did I know, my actions had not gone unnoticed. As it turns out, the JV coaches had been reporting back to the head coach about my play. They convinced him to give me a shot. Going into the last game of the year, I was informed that I would be starting with the varsity defense. I had given up on the idea that I would get much playing time that year, and now I was going to be starting. To say I was excited would be an understatement.

As I took the field, I couldn't help but think about the entire year – all the games I played with the younger kids and all the fun I had. None of that would have happened if I had just quit. I had focused not just on myself, but on helping the younger players get better. Because of that, I was now standing on the field in front of my entire school as a starter.

As the game began, I took a moment to take it all in. The butterflies, the energy, the exhilaration – they're still etched into my mind to this day. And I remember, as my eyes scanned the stands, scanning the blur of faces of those who came to watch the game, one face suddenly became clear. It was the face of my dad cheering me on. It was the first time in three years anyone had ever come to watch me play. And play is just what I did.

The following year, my senior year, to my surprise I was

unanimously voted captain of the football team. I played a lot that last year, playing both offense and defense the entire season. I never expected to be captain of the team, nor did I expect that I would be nominated to play in the state all-star game, the only representative from my school. But that is the funny thing about expectations: Sometimes they don't live up to what you thought they'd be, and other times they far surpass them.

Nothing I accomplished in sports would have been possible had I not embraced the idea of doing what I loved rather than trying to live up to some self-created expectation. And what empowered me while I was playing was my focus on elevating those around me. I didn't want to just succeed for myself, I wanted to succeed by helping those around me. And, in turn, by helping others get better, I got better, too.

Now, in the interest of full disclosure, doing for others can have a few risks associated with it. But if you approach this with the correct mindset, the risks are far outweighed by the rewards.

The big pushback I always hear regarding doing for others is the idea that if you always do for others, you won't have anything left for yourself. I am here to tell you that, yes, there can be a risk involved in helping others too much. It is possible to do too much for others, especially if it is done to your own detriment. But that doesn't mean you shouldn't do it.

I am a huge fan of giving to others of my time, my money, my efforts, and my love. But I'm also very careful to not give so much that I cannot support myself. For if I can't take care of me, there will be no me left to take care of others.

A perfect example of this is illustrated in the talk given before a flight.

If you've ever flown anywhere, you know that every airline gives the same pre-flight instructions. It goes something like this:

> *In the unlikely event of change in cabin pressure, oxygen masks will drop down from above. Place the mask over your mouth and breathe regularly. If you are traveling with small children*

or someone that requires your assistance, please make sure to put on your mask first before assisting others.

Why do they tell you this? Is it because they are selfish and think you should be selfish, too? No, it's because if you are laying on the floor unconscious from lack of oxygen, you can't help the other people that need your help.

It's the same thing with kindness. If you are not kind to yourself first, you will not be able to be kind to others.

For years, I was not kind to myself. In fact, I hated the person I was. But I had this belief that if I could be kind to everyone else that it would somehow make me a more valuable person. And while that did happen in a way, it never changed how I saw myself. No matter how many people saw me as kind and generous, I never saw myself that way. No matter what I did for others, it never felt like it was enough. And when I did try to do something for myself, the guilt was so bad it outweighed all the good I had done in my mind.

Until I really learned to love myself, I wasn't much good to the people around me, especially to those closest to me. My guilt, self-loathing, and pain often materialized as anger and frustration. I wasn't a very good friend, a good son, or a good husband or father for many years. I often did more for strangers than for my own family. When I would do something for family, it was often begrudgingly done with attitude and annoyance.

I could see it and feel it in myself and in the faces of those I loved most. This only caused more guilt and pain, continuing that cycle and making things worse.

If you are reading this, and you were someone who was close to me, I'm sorry. I know I was a shit for many years. I hope by now I've personally apologized to you for it, but if not, please know I am sorry.

Another risk associated with giving can be when you allow yourself to be taken advantage of by others. There are people out in the world that I like to call "takers." Takers are people who do nothing but take from you; they take your time, your energy, your love, your kindness, and your resources. Very rarely do these people give back to you, and, when they do, it is usually so they can take even more in the future.

These people, while they should always be treated with love and respect, should be recognized as unhealthy people in our lives. Takers are not looking out for you. They are only looking out for themselves. What makes them so unhealthy is that they see your kindness as weakness, and they'll often manipulate you to get what they want. Eventually, you will become so drained by these people that you will have nothing left for yourself.

Even worse, these people can be anyone from a stranger, to your best friend, or even a close family member. Trying to manage a relationship with someone who is a taker can be very challenging, but it is possible. It simply requires you to have a strong self-value and self-confidence to face their pushback when they don't get what they want from you.

And while these people don't necessarily need to be cut out of your life entirely, until you are in a healthy place for yourself, you should limit your interaction with these types of people. At least until you learn to say the all-important "no," which is not easy for people who like to take care of others. Learning to say no to things that do not serve you isn't a selfish act, it's a self-care act.

Takers will make you feel like you are not doing enough for them. They will play on your guilt and your emotions to make you feel like you need to do more for them than you currently are doing. But the catch is, there is never enough you can do because they will always want a little bit more. That is why learning to say no is such a loving thing for your self and for them. Why is saying no loving for them? Because it will force them into a situation that will require dealing with why they take in the first place. Those who never say no to people in their lives end up enabling behavior that can be detrimental. Enabling behavior is a term used in recovery circles to discuss the action someone takes that allow the unhealthy or self-destructive behavior to continue. Giving money to someone who uses it to buy drugs or alcohol, making excuses for abusive outbursts, accepting inappropriate behavior, or always cleaning up their mess are all examples of enabling behavior. This does not help someone get better rather it allows him or her to avoid facing the issues causing the action. Learning to say no to someone you love, especially someone in pain, is never easy. But it could be the only thing that will push him or her towards fixing what is broken about their life.

So you may be wondering, "If I'm doing something for someone else to make myself feel better, what is the difference between me and a taker?"

Well, I'm not telling you to do something with the expectation of making yourself feel better. I'm telling you that doing something for someone else makes you feel better. There is a difference. And that difference is significant.

If you attach an expectation to an act of kindness, you immediately increase the chances that you will cause more suffering in your life. Expectations are very rarely ever met the way we want them to be. It is, in fact, the expectations we place on everything in our lives that cause the majority of our suffering.

Acts of kindness are no different.

If I do something nice for someone else, I do it with no expectation of anything in return. Often I do it anonymously so that there can be no response. This is because the act of doing for someone else is enough. I don't expect anything in return, so I can never be disappointed by the response.

Always put the focus on the goal and the action you take, rather than the result. You can't change the result of things but you can change your actions. If you do not like the results you are getting, change what you're doing.

One of the biggest issues I had while dealing with anxiety was to try and manipulate the results first. I would picture in my head the result I wanted. I would then try to create the action that I believed would generate that desired result. Inevitably, the result would not match my expectation, and I would get frustrated.

This happened most frequently within my personal relationships with my parents as I got older. Holidays were especially a challenging time for us all. When we were younger, the court order often dictated how we split up the visitation around the holidays. They alternated whose house we were at for which holiday year after year.

But as each of us got older, got married, and had children of our own, making plans around the holidays became especially difficult. I always wanted everyone to be happy, so I would attempt to agree to everything from everyone. I would double-book my days, causing me to always feel rushed, trying to visit multiple places in a single day. Instead of making people happy, it made people feel like they were all low on my priority list, since I was only staying with them for a part of the day and then leaving to go to another party or event.

Eventually, I began to pull back from all events. The stress and the hurt feelings were too much, and I began pushing everyone away. If I couldn't go everywhere and see everyone, I didn't want to go anywhere.

This pattern of trying to control the outcome repeated over and over again in my life until I began to recognize it. But to be honest, I still catch myself looking past the action and toward the result. Habits are difficult to break, especially when they are easily triggered.

This book is a perfect example of how challenging it can be to break old patterns and habits. I struggled at times with finishing this book because I've looked past the action and on to what may result from it being finished. The dream of being able to say that I'm a published author causes me to lose focus and limits my ability to take action. As the action slows down, so does my confidence in being able to reach my goal.

Only by refocusing on my action, taking time each day to write, would this book ever be finished. Once it's been written, whatever results could come from it are outside my control. I can't guarantee it will be published or that anyone will ever read it. I can only control the action I take, which has been writing each day, completing the book, and making it available for others.

This does not mean you should take action without knowing what you are working toward. This is, in many ways, a very counterproductive and wasteful way to work. Taking action for the sake of doing something is just busywork. Sometimes it can accidentally move you forward, but most times, it simply just keeps you moving and eventually wears you out. Without knowing your destination, movement does not guarantee you will ever get where you want to go.

What I am saying is that there is a difference between results and goals.

The best way to avoid feeling disappointed in an unrealized expectation or result is to focus on a goal rather than a result. Some people use these two words interchangeably, but this is how I define them: A goal is a target to aim for, something you would like to accomplish. A result is the byproduct of what happens after your goal is achieved.

Any time I move toward creating something in my life, I apply three simple steps:

Step 1: Know the goal.

Step 2: Plan the actions.

Step 3: Be open to the results.

Let me give you an example.

When I made the decision that I wanted to help as many people as I could to learn to manage anxiety, fear, and worry, I set a goal to write a book about my experience. Once I knew what my goal was, I worked backward to figure out what actions I had to take in order to get the book written.

That action, of course, was to start writing. The plan around that action could vary based on what worked best for me. I could choose to write a small amount each day. I could write in large chunks spread out over each week. Or I could write in really large chunks for a small time in order to finish quickly. I opted to write small amounts each day over a longer period of time.

The writing is the action that I needed to take in order to complete the book. I know that my goal is to finish the book, but the results of what happens after the book is written is unknown.

If I started by focusing on the results I wanted, I would most likely end up disappointed in the end. Let's say I wanted the result of writing my book to be that it helps millions of people improve their lives, but after the book is written, that does not happen. I would be disappointed in my book because I did not achieve my desired result: helping millions of people. But by focusing on simply reaching the goal of completing the book, I can be proud of my accomplishment regardless of what happens as a result of my reaching it.

This does not mean that I don't want my book to do well or to help people. It simply means that by focusing on achieving my goal of writing the book, I will have a greater sense of happiness and accomplishment when it is completed. And any results will be positive.

My goal is to give and to help others. My action is to write this book so that others may benefit from what I've learned and experienced. When your actions and goals are aligned with the desire to help others, you will experience a feeling of fulfillment that is pursued by many but achieved by few.

"Mastering others is strength. Mastering yourself is true power."
– **Lao Tzu**

CHAPTER 8: DISCOVERING THE CORE OF YOUR ANXIETY

Through years of self-reflection trying to understand my anxiety, I've learned that many of the negative patterns that have controlled my adult life originated from those fights between my parents and the lasting effect they had on me. How they made me feel about myself caused me to question everything about who I was and what type of value I had.

Children have a strange way of internalizing situations, especially the ones regarding their parents. When negative things happen and children are at a loss to understand why, they blame themselves. I guess in some way I blamed myself for my parents' divorce. Their anger always seemed to eventually become directed at my older brother and me. My parents got mad at each other and then they yelled at us. And while I know now their anger wasn't directed toward us intentionally, their actions cause me to internalize what was happening and feel as if I had done something or not done something, to deserve their anger. This not knowing what I was doing left me with a fear of doing the wrong things or making mistakes. I had to be perfect, or I wouldn't do it at all. If I were unclear of a choice, I wouldn't decide. Eventually, I would convince myself I lacked the ability to make the correct choice, so I stopped making them, or I made the one that made me feel the safest.

Each time something came up that required me to make a choice, I would struggle with taking action. I never knew how to start projects because I spent so much time going back and forth over all the elements that needed to be discussed or addressed prior to taking action.

I worried about making the wrong choice. I would play out every possible scenario in my mind, always focused on which one would turn out the least horrible. Less suffering seemed to be the goal with me. I didn't choose things I wanted to do, I chose things I thought would make everyone else happiest.

When I did have an idea about what I wanted to do, instead of just going for it, I would go over every possible scenario for how it could go wrong or why I should do the exact opposite. I often talked myself out of doing things I felt I should do. My gut told me yes, but my mind would eventually tell me no. Because of this, I often chose not to take action on things I felt drawn to do. This kept me from moving forward and often left me feeling stuck in the same place. Being in the same place meant I didn't have to make a choice. Familiar became safe.

I began to fear change. I had already gone through quite a bit in my life. Any new change would just bring more pain.

The start of each school year was traumatic for me. A new teacher and a new classroom meant uncertainty and fear. The last month of my summer vacations were always incredibly stressful.

I didn't want to go back to school. I didn't want to face change. I felt sick to my stomach over getting on that bus, going into a new room, and dealing with a new situation.

I wanted to freeze the hands of time. I wanted nothing to ever change. I desired things to be as they always were, even if they were unpleasant. I would rather stay in a bad situation forever than take a chance on making it better by risking my comfort.

But life does not stand still for anyone. Time continues to move forward, and I felt as if I was dragged into my future, kicking and screaming – sometimes quite literally.

My mom did her best to deal with the situation. She would call the school each year and make arrangements for me to come in and meet my teacher before anyone else. I could check out the classroom, get a feel for the room, and try to put some of my fears at ease.

It helped a little, but it never really seemed to make the stress and worry go away completely. It was always there.

I was one of the few children at school whose parents were divorced. This made me feel different from the rest of the kids. I felt like everyone knew my family wasn't like theirs and looked at me differently because of it. It felt as if everyone's eyes were always on me, watching and judging me for what I did, who I was, and how my family acted.

It didn't help that I was also a very emotional child. When I felt something, I wasn't very good at hiding it. I wore my emotions on my sleeve. It wasn't unheard of for me to cry when I got upset. I just couldn't control it.

Once in fourth grade, I was having a hard time with a spelling test. For some reason, I kept spelling the word "farther" wrong. I'd write "father," without the first "r." (Being from Massachusetts, we're famous for dropping our Rs from words when we talk. You know, the old "pahk the cah in the Hahvahd yahd" saying.) I knew the word was "farther," but I kept pronouncing it "fah*ther.*"

I got very emotional in class and felt frustrated. I couldn't understand why I was spelling the word wrong. The teacher called me up to her desk and tried to help me. She asked me to sound it out and to think about the letters and the sounds. I tried. I failed. I cried.

Then my teacher asked me something that I still hear echoing in my head. She asked, "Are you upset because your *father* is *farther* away?"

I'm not exactly sure what she was trying to accomplish by asking me this question, but in a strange way she was right. I was upset that my father was farther away. I wanted him to be closer. I wanted him to live in my house instead of me having to go visit him at his. I wanted to see him every day when I went home. I wanted him to ask me how school was. I wanted him to teach me how to spell words like "farther" and to comfort me when I couldn't.

I felt powerless in my own life. I had no control over the situation that had gone on in my family. I wanted to fix it. I wanted to make my parents happy and bring them back together. I felt frustrated and angry because I couldn't do any of those things. I couldn't do anything. I couldn't even spell "farther."

All that emotion and pain was coming out in that moment, in the middle of school and in front of all my classmates.

My teacher did her best to calm me down. She explained to me why I was spelling the word wrong. I immediately felt embarrassed. Everyone was looking at me. Everyone saw me lose it over a spelling word, even though it wasn't just about a word for me.

I walked back to my desk, wiping the tears from my eyes with my shirt sleeve. I could feel the eyes of all my classmates pierce my skin with each step. I didn't dare look at anyone. I just stared at my feet and returned to my seat. If I could have crawled under my desk and hid, I would have. I never wanted to feel this way again.

Sadly, this would mark the beginning of a change for me.

In that one moment, my mind seemed to connect that feeling of embarrassment with failing and getting upset. I tried to spell that word, and I couldn't do it. I wanted to spell it, and it was frustrating that I couldn't. That caused all those other emotions to bubble up to the surface and make the situation even worse. Instead of seeing that failure as a step on the path of learning to spell the word correctly, I saw it as a humiliation that made me feel vulnerable and exposed.

I never wanted to feel that way again, so I never wanted to fail again. And the best way for me to never fail again seemed simple: Stop trying.

This fear of failure has plagued me my entire adult life. Even today as I write this book, I find myself suffering at times from imposter syndrome. I worry that people will not like the book, that it will be viewed as too simplistic or obvious, and that someone like me has no business even writing a book. If I never write this book, I can never be viewed as a failure if this book doesn't do well. But I also know that if I do not write this book, I have already failed. Even worse, there may be someone out there who would have benefitted from hearing my story, someone who needs to hear what I have to say.

My friend and writer Michael J. Chase, author of the books *Am I Being Kind*, *The Radical Practice of Loving Everyone*, and *Truth Over Shame*, once told me, "Sometimes you are writing your book, and sometimes you are living your book."

Everything that I put into the pages of this book I have lived and continue to live. There is nothing here that I don't practice and apply to my life daily. I wouldn't share these with you if I didn't learn from them first and continue to benefit from them each day.

Bits of advice and guidance from friends like Michael have helped me understand things about myself and allowed me to look at my life in a way that has become eye opening. When you shed your fear of failure, you allow yourself to look upon your life with a strange permission to be honest and brutal in a very loving and noncritical way.

I've developed the ability to see that events from my childhood – like the one with my teacher over my spelling word – have played out over and over again in my mind. Every time I sat in a meeting at work, my forehead covered in sweat at the idea of being singled out or called upon to speak, there was a small part of that little boy still inside, reliving the embarrassment and pain. That moment was not simply born from the instance of not being able to spell "farther" in front of my classmates, but from the pain buried within the idea that I couldn't resolve or forgive myself over my parents' divorce.

That is the tricky thing about our experiences. Sometimes it's easy to connect the dots between our pain and our experiences, but other times those dots are far more hidden.

Many of the events we experience in life – the good and the bad, the happy and the sad – all contribute to our perspective of the world. We use the information we see, hear, and feel to join our experiences. As we get older, our brains recall this information to help us make decisions. Sometimes this is done on a conscious level and other times it's on a subconscious level.

Not every moment we experience has a lasting impact. After all, I spent thousands of days sitting in classrooms in my lifetime. Many of those moments I cannot recall who was there or what I was or wasn't doing.

So why does this particular moment in class stand out to me? Why did it have such a lasting impact on me while so many other moments have simply faded into obscurity? In truth, I don't have a very good memory at all. Much of it is because of my anxiety.

When I'm introduced to someone for the first time, as he would be telling me his name, I'd be so fixated on if I was sweating or fumbling through the introduction, I wouldn't actually hear the name he told me. It wasn't as if I couldn't remember the name, but I was so distracted by my anxious thoughts, I couldn't focus to remember it.

As it turns out, there are a few ways to commit something to memory. One way is through repetition. I can repeat something over and over again until it's committed to memory, much like when I would study for a test in school. I would repeat words or sometimes put them into a song or rhyme to help recall facts for a test. This process of memorization is called a mnemonic device. It's a way of coding the brain to better remember the information to be used at a later time.

But there is another way to create a lasting memory that doesn't require tricks or techniques. It's the natural process our minds use to decide which memories will stick with you over the years and which ones will fade into the background of your life. It's a simple formula and requires two parts..

The first is the experience itself. Experiences happen every second of every day. Each moment we exist, we are experiencing something. Even if it is a silent moment, it's still an experience. But most of us are not able to recall every second of every day. It would simply be too much for our brains to keep straight and we'd go into information overload. So our brain has to be more selective about what information it takes in and stores for the long-term.

In order for most people to make a long-lasting memory, there needs to be a second element, which is an elevated emotional state at the time of the experience. When an experience is combined with a highly emotional state, the details of the event become indelibly etched into our minds, often with striking detail.

This is why most people in the United States can easily recall the exact moments of where they were when certain major events happened, such as the assassination of President John F. Kennedy or the attacks of 9/11. Most people can remember where they were and what they were doing when they became aware of the planes striking the twin towers the morning of September 11, 2001. But most of them would be hard-pressed to recall what they were doing on the morning of September 10.

When an event or experience is coupled with an elevated emotional state, there is a far better chance that you will remember that moment in great detail. And emotional states can be elevated in many different ways. Excitement, joy, surprise, sadness, fear, or pain can all work to cement an experience into our subconscious minds. When we are really young, our parents try to teach us things to keep us safe. As a parent myself, I often find myself telling my children things I hope will save them from either physical or emotional pain. But often we need to be exposed to that emotional pain in order for the lesson to really stick.

Here's an example. I feel as though I've spent years' worth of my life telling my children not to touch items that get hot, everything from the burners on the stove to our fireplace to the light fixtures in our home.

One evening while we were on vacation on Cape Cod, we were busily getting the kids ready for bed. On the nightstand next to my daughter's bed was a lamp in the shape of a lighthouse. It had a white shade covered with anchors and other nautical symbols. It was low and well within her reach. Now, I had told her multiple times to never touch the light bulbs in lamps because they were very hot. Yet, no matter how many times I had told her this, that night she reached out and pressed her thumb inexplicably on to the light bulb of the glowing lamp.

In an instant, before I could get a single word out of my mouth, she pulled back in excruciating pain. Her thumb immediately turned a bright shade of red, and the tears quickly followed. I said what generation after generation of parents said to their children after doing something like this: "Honey, how many times have I told you not to touch the light because it's hot?!"

To this day, my daughter still talks about the time she burned her thumb on that light. She is very cautious around items that get hot and is extra protective of both of her younger brothers regarding safety.

No matter how many times she had been verbally warned about not touching things that were hot, it took the physical pain – which elevated her emotional state – for that lesson to sink in and become something she can now quickly recall with almost no effort.

And I could easily relate to her pain, because the moment she burned her thumb on that light bulb, the memory of pressing my thumb to a cigarette lighter in my father's truck when I was a young boy instantly appeared in my mind. It took zero effort to recall that sympathetic moment in my mind because the lesson had been so permanently etched into my memory, much like that lamp has been etched into hers.

The mind is such an amazing piece of technology. It functions on a level that we hardly can imagine or begin to understand. But the advances that have been made in recent years regarding how our minds work have opened new doors and changed what we once thought regarding our ability to think, to reason, and, more importantly, to change.

So what does burning our thumbs and being embarrassed in front of our classmates have to do with anxiety, fear, and changing our lives? Quite a lot, as it turns out.

They say that success leaves clues. Many people who study some of the world's most successful entrepreneurs and business owners often talk about how you can learn a lot from the strategies and tactics used by these people to become successful. In other words, you can look at the clues their success has left behind and then apply those same actions and disciplines to your own life or business in an attempt to recreate their success.

The same can be said about anxiety. Your anxious feeling in response to things in the world is a direct result of what you've learned, experienced, and been told; the way you've been treated and been made to feel by others; and your desire to avoid or repeat those situations.

The challenging part is figuring out what things happened that caused you to respond this way as you got older. Trying to piece together the clues of your own life to solve the mystery of your anxiety is no easy task, especially for those who struggle with low self-esteem or an overinflated attachment to their ego.

We all have a tendency to want to protect ourselves from things that cause us to feel uncomfortable. For those of us suffering from anxiety, this tendency is unnaturally inflated by our unrealistic fears. We go to great lengths to avoid feeling discomfort, both physically and emotionally. We want to protect ourselves from experiencing any more pain, so we go to great lengths to avoid the exposure. This can start as a conscious choice, like the feeling of not really wanting to go out with friends. Eventually, it can manifest itself into real, physical issues that we blame for our inability to do things.

So how do we go about figuring out where our anxiety comes from? Well, it's simple, but it's far from easy. I've found there are three steps you need to take in order to make this happen.

Step One: Dig Deep to Find Your Pain

This is the point where I usually refer people to speak to a licensed therapist. It's also the point people often smile and say, "I don't need to see a shrink, but thanks anyway!"

There is a horrible stigma attached to therapy or seeking any help for a mental disorder like anxiety or depression. I'm proud to say I have spoken to therapists on many occasions. In fact, I continue to go back every once in a while just to check in. I've found men in particular have a difficult time seeing a therapist or even just being willing to talk about our emotions. (I could write an entire book on men trying to deal with their emotions. We have been taught by society that we are supposed to be strong, tough, and problem-solvers. But we fool ourselves into thinking we can solve everything on our own.)

Here's a real "guy" way of thinking about therapy: If your car breaks down, you take it to a mechanic, right? Well, think of a therapist as a mechanic for your mind. If you are willing to pop the hood of your emotions, a good therapist can get your mind running much more efficiently.

Now, if you happen to be someone who can take a hard look at yourself and be brutally honest with how you feel, you may be able to dig into your own emotional baggage and figure out what is causing your anxiety. But most people struggle to do this on their own because they are too close to their own life to see it from the proper perspective. An outsider can often see things much quicker and more clearly because they don't have the subconscious defenses built in. We often try to protect ourselves by unknowingly altering how we see the experiences of our life. Facades we've created can easily blind us because we choose to let them, but an outsider can challenge those beliefs in a way that causes us to be honest with ourself.

Think about it: Isn't it always so much easier to see what other people should do to fix their lives, but we struggle to fix our own? We can see other people's problems with a much clearer view because we are not concerned with protecting ourselves from what the solution might require. We can tell others how to fix their life with ease, but struggle mightily with fixing our own life because we are far too close to our own problems. So speaking to a therapist, while uncomfortable at first, is often the quickest and most effective way to get past the illusion you've created and address the core of your issues.

And when you're finding a therapist, it is critical you find one you feel comfortable with, because you need to be willing to open up to him or her. If you are not honest with your therapist, you are not being honest with yourself. What is worse is that you might not even be aware you aren't being honest. We often fool ourselves – again for self-preservation – by lying about how we feel and what we remember about our past. We want to protect the memories we have, the people who mean the most to us, and the history of our lives, because we identify with that story as part of who we are. To open up about something that is painful requires us to be vulnerable, and that is counter to our ego-driven, survivalist mindset that wants to keep us safe and alive.

A good therapist will lead you down the road to understanding things about yourself that you simply can't do on your own. They are trained to know what to ask and to help you process your answers. But keep in mind, their job isn't to give you the answers. Good therapists aren't there to solve your problems. They are there to get you to see your problems and help empower you with the tools to solve them yourself.

Learning to open up about our pain is a major step in the healing process. Some people can do it alone, but it is often something that is easier to do with the guidance and support of someone specially trained to deal with what will come once the floodgates open and the healing begins.

Now, if you are set against speaking to a therapist, at least be willing and open to asking yourself some tough questions. You'll need to dig deep into areas you don't want to go. You must be willing to open doors you've closed countless years ago. You closed them for a reason. That reason is because part of you felt you'd be better off moving on and pretending these events never happened. I can honestly tell you, from personal experience, this is not the case. Your anxiety is here because you've never dealt with these things. And the only way it will really begin to subside permanently is if you are willing to heal those wounds rather than just pretend they are not there.

You must be willing to peek in the deepest, darkest corners of your mind. This is why this is often referred to as shadow work, because it's made up of looking for what you've hidden in the shadow of your mind. And the best way to remove a shadow is to bring it into the light! And this leads us to the second step of the process.

Step Two: Healing the Pain Means Feeling the Pain

If you thought you'd get out of this experience without shedding a tear or two – or two hundred – you are mistaken. Learning to open up to our emotions requires us to experience the feelings those emotions are made of. You cannot deal with the feelings of sadness or loss without allowing yourself to feel them. Often, our anxiety is the fear repeating something that brings up those feelings. Our inability to process these feelings is the actual core of the anxiety. Avoiding things that make us feel uncomfortable is a natural reaction but it's one you need to address. Every successful person in life has experienced feeling uncomfortable at one time or another. What makes those who are successful stand out from everyone else is that, instead of ignoring those feelings by avoiding the situation, they embraced and acknowledged those feelings and pushed forward anyway.

So much of our hidden pain comes from the fact that, when we experienced something that was emotionally damaging in our past, we didn't know how to process it. Because we didn't have the proper tools to process these emotions in a healthy way, we unknowingly created an unhealthy response to them. It can be to deny the feeling or emotion, to counteract it with defensiveness or aggressive behavior, to soothe the emotion through external stimuli such as alcohol, drugs, sex, eating or video games, or to simply avoid anyone or anything that causes the emotion to surface in the first place.

For many years, I used alcohol to compensate for my emotional feelings of abandonment and not feeling like I was worthy of being loved. Whenever something got too overwhelming, I would turn to alcohol. Drinking gave me a temporary reprieve from my feelings. It gave me courage to face things I was afraid to face, to say things I was afraid to say, and to do things I was afraid to do. The source of that fear was that I didn't want to be rejected or made to feel unloved. Because I didn't want to feel rejected, I needed to become a people-pleaser. Everything I did was for everyone else. I needed them to like me, to think good things about me, and to not judge me. But when I drank, I didn't care about those things anymore. I was able to say what I wanted. I felt brave when I was drunk. It was the only time I felt what I had defined as "normal." The truth was, I didn't love myself, so I always worried others wouldn't love me either. The drinking covered the emotional pain of feeling unwanted.

Had I simply dealt with my drinking, but never dealt with my emotional pain, my success would have been short-lived. The desire to drink would have still been there because the emotional pain it masked would have still been there. Every day would be a struggle because the desire to drink would have simply been replaced with the willpower to not drink. At some point, my willpower would have given way to my desire. But since I faced and removed the pain that caused the desire, that desire is no longer there. And when there is no desire to do something, willpower is not required to avoid doing it.

This is why it is key to uncover the source of the pain that feeds the desire of your anxiety. As long as that core pain is still present, so, too, will your anxiety be present. If you have anxiety and fear, you are in pain. You need to heal that pain. The only way to heal it is to feel it. You must own your pain. Allow yourself the pain and suffering that is associated with such things. Don't judge yourself for feeling it. Don't look down or criticize yourself. Don't tell yourself you are weak or damaged.

Feeling pain requires strength. It is far easier to pretend you are not hurt than to allow yourself to be hurt. There is great strength in vulnerability. When you learn you can be vulnerable and remain powerful, that is the definition of true strength. It is a strength no low point can ever take from you. It is yours, and it will forever be there, waiting to help you rise and overcome any obstacle life has to offer.

Step Three: Repeat Steps One and Two as Often as Required

This process doesn't really ever stop. If it did, it would mean you had stopped living. Each day, the things we experience impact our lives, our emotions, and our minds. They become part of us and our stories.

The more you become consciously aware of how you interact with each of these moments, the more deeply you'll embrace each moment from a place of pure joy and bliss. But to fully become consciously aware, you must first purify the lens in which you see the world around you. You must learn to let go of the pain that blocks how you experience your life and open your eyes, your mind, and your heart to all that your life has to offer.

Things do not happen to you, they happen with you. You are either the conscious creator of your life or its unconscious creator. When you are unconscious to your part in creating your life, it feels as if life is happening to you. You feel like the victim and often feel out of control.

But when you awaken that deeper understanding of the role you play in creating your own life, through healing your emotional pain, the world opens up and becomes a place full of wonder and opportunity. A place you can create and enjoy, free of fear and full of love.

"We don't rise to the level of our expectations, we fall to the level of our training."
– Archilochus

CHAPTER 9:
PRACTICE WITH INTENTION

When I was growing up, I loved movies. Any story that allowed me to escape my reality and get lost temporarily in the adventures of another person was a welcomed distraction. Some of my favorites were *Star Wars, Indiana Jones, ET the Extra Terrestrial, Gremlins,* and *The Goonies,* just to name a few.

So when I found myself living in a new town, faced with the prospect of making friends at the age of thirteen, it's no wonder that I would have relied on the wisdom of movies to offer me the solution to my problems.

The wisest sage I had been exposed to in my life at that time was Yoda, the lovable Jedi Master from the *Star Wars* movies. But since the chances of me becoming a Jedi and learning to use the force seemed a bit unrealistic, I had to go with the second wisest guru I knew, Mr. Miyagi, from the movie *The Karate Kid*.

The Karate Kid was one of my favorite films growing up. To be honest, I still kind of love it. How can you not love the story of an outsider who moves to a new town, gets bullied by karate-kicking high school kids, befriends a maintenance man, learns karate in two months, beats the bullies, wins the karate tournament, earns his respect, and gets the girl?

Maybe it wasn't the most realistic movie ever made, but for someone who suffered from anxiety and always felt like an outsider in his own skin, there was something I could relate to in this story. Plus, I just really loved karate movies.

So the fact that my new town had a karate studio in the center of town seemed like a sign that this was what I needed to do.

I asked my father if I could take lessons. One thing you learn really early on growing up in a divorced environment is which parent to approach first when asking for something. My father was also a fan of karate movies, plus being a police officer he understood the benefit of self-defense. His only rule was that I had to stick with it for longer than five minutes. I couldn't start and then quit if I didn't like it. I had to agree to give it a few months to see if it was something I'd enjoy. I agreed to the terms with ease. After all, this was going to be different. I was going to be a karate master. Of this I had no doubt.

I quickly realized that what you see in movies and what goes on in an actual class are quite different.

Instead of learning high-flying, spinning back kicks, I was learning how to stand, how to step, and how to do basic blocks and punches. Everything seemed foreign, forced, and awkward. None of the motions were anything like the overdramatized kicks and punches my friends and I had thrown in our backyards, and I was definitely not being taught the secret "crane technique" Daniel used to best Johnny and win the Under 18 All Valley Karate Championship!

But nevertheless, I had committed to sticking it out a few months, and that is what I did. Soon, weeks became months and what felt very foreign and awkward in the beginning started to feel natural and familiar. I had learned how to do the basic blocks, strikes, and kicks. I had practiced them over and over again, each week the same as the last.

I was about six months in and starting to lose interest when something happened that caught me completely by surprise. Literally.

I was in class with my friends, talking and hanging out, when someone in the back of the class dropped a very large book. The sound echoed through the room unexpectedly. Everyone jumped up in fear, completely unaware of what had happened. I jumped as well. But when we all caught our breath, I realized that my reaction was different from my friends' response.

I looked at all my friends and noticed each one of them, upon hearing the noise, jumped back with their hands either out by their sides or grasping at their chests. When I looked down at myself, I was standing in what is called an "on-guard" stance, which I had learned in karate class. I had my right foot forward and my left foot back. My hands were up in a defensive position, ready to offer protection from whatever caused that noise.

Because it had happened without any advanced warning, none of us had any time to consciously think about how to react to the situation. In that moment, each one of us reacted from our subconscious mind, a sort of autopilot. Our bodies simply responded without conscious thought. But my reaction was not the same as everyone else. My body had moved into the exact position I had been practicing for months. But the amazing part was that I didn't have to think about putting myself in that position. My mind reacted from a place of subconscious memory, learned through repetitive action.

I had practiced all those basic moves so often that they had become ingrained into my subconscious mind and body. Through simple repetition, I had taught my mind and body to respond without the need for conscious thought. And when faced with a scenario that seemed threatening, it responded in kind.

I think back on this moment often in my everyday interactions. So much of my life has been practicing and learning through repetition, allowing my mind and body to respond without my conscious thought as to how or why. The only difference is that instead of using blocks, punches, and kicks to defend itself, my body was using anxiety, panic, and fear as a way to prepare and avoid things that were threatening.

My anxiety had become my body's way of defending itself on a subconscious level. After all, what better way to avoid something bad from happening than by not being there? Through all my years of experiencing those emotions, behaviors, and actions associated with anxiety, I had become an anxiety master! My body no longer needed my conscious mind to control things because my subconscious mind was in control. It had taken over my body and, in turn, taken over my life.

But how did this happen and, more importantly, how do we reverse things and learn to take back control from our subconscious mind?

By using the same exact process we used when we created our anxiety in the first place. We have to practice.

Practice is the process of learning and understanding through repetitive motion or action. Everything in the physical world takes time. Time is the way of measuring things as they happen, and anything that is happening is changing. If nothing changed, nothing would be happening. As things grow, move, think, breathe, age, or any other action that can be done, change is created. Something is altered from one moment to the next. Change is happening at every moment, by everything. Change is constant.

The Greek philosopher Heraclitus said that the only constant is change. This is true. Everything in the universe is changing at every moment. We are no exception. Every action we take, every experience we witness, every conversation we have, every person we meet, and every thought that we entertain in some way shifts and changes who we are, shaping and molding our beliefs and our perspective of the world. Each time we think a similar thought again and again, we strengthen our hold on that as something that is real or true in our reality. So, as we think things repetitively, we are actually practicing to have that thought with more ease.

When we then take that idea or thought and place action behind it, we are practicing to turn that non-physical idea into a physical manifestation of our world. And make no mistake: You can manifest a physical thing into the world simply through your thoughts. Your thoughts are incredibly powerful ideas that can change your physical body and experiences. This is why learning to understand and control your thoughts is such a critical part of overcoming anxiety, fear, and worry. Negative thinking is a way of practicing for an outcome you don't want.

The trouble is that without even knowing you were doing it, you've been practicing the art of negative thinking, worrying, and being anxious for years. You've been programming your mind to become an anxiety machine. And you've done this through the art of practice.

What we want to do now is to understand that this has been happening and use this tool to create something you want – love – rather than create something you don't want – fear.

Being able to practice is a way of taking something you know and applying it to your daily life. It is critical to learning, growing, and living. We practice all of the time. Everything we've ever learned has been put into practice so that we can develop the skills to make it reality. Without practice, these things would simply be thought forms – or theories.

Most everything we do is a practice. Even something as simple as getting out of bed had to be learned and practiced. As a baby, you didn't have the strength or physical dexterity to roll, crawl, sit, or stand. You had to practice these skills in order to learn them. Once you did, you progressed to standing within your crib and crying to get out. Still, you had not learned the skills required to get out of your own bed yet. As you continued to grow, you eventually learned how to climb out of your own crib. This was usually the sign for your parents to switch from a crib to a bed, so you didn't tumble onto the floor.

As an adult, you now give very little thought to getting out of bed in the morning. You do not think about all the muscles required to power your body up and into action each day. It just comes naturally. For most, the greatest obstacle in getting out of bed is a cold floor, a negative attitude, or a crippling fear that something bad is waiting for you, so it's better to just stay under the covers. But remember that one time in your life, you had the goal to be able to physically get out of your bed. You focused your intention on achieving this goal. You practiced developing the skills that would allow you to achieve this goal – and you achieved it.

So what is the difference between practicing something you want and practicing something you don't want? The answer is your intention.

We practice things each and every day, but we do not always have intention behind what we practice. As we live unconscious lives, our practices also become unconscious. Coming home from work, sitting in front of the television, and watching the news is a practice. People learn this, and eventually it becomes second nature. Most people don't even realize that they do this anymore because they've become such a master of this skill that, much like getting out of bed, it has become a part of them.

What if you could see the good in others, be happy, and love your life and everything about it? What if you could smile and be grateful every day without having to think about it? To just be the kind of person that inspires happiness in others? Most people would love for that to become their reality. And it can. All you need to do is to consciously set your intention on becoming that way and then practice the skills and habits that support this type of lifestyle. This is practicing with intention.

As you learn to practice with intention, you will see the power it has. Some of us already practice with intention, while others practice unconsciously. What it means to practice unconsciously is that we have patterns or habits in our lives that we are unaware of. Some of these are good habits, but some of these aren't. A habit is something you do over and over again; you'll notice this is also the definition of a practice. So, when you have a habit that is bad, you are actually practicing to learn a bad action within your life.

Please understand, when I say "bad," I do not mean it in an evil or even a negative way. I simply mean to describe an action or habit that is not fully planned, intended, or serving you in a positive way. Some habits that we create unconsciously would be considered "good" habits to have. I merely aim to point out that if you want to gain control over your life and the direction it is going, you need to be aware of what actions you are creating through your daily practice or habits.

There are many steps to understanding what life you want to create. You must first understand what that life will look like by being honest with yourself about the motivations behind what you want. Once you understand what you want your life to look like, you must learn what it is you need to do on a daily basis to enable you to create that life. Finally, you must practice those actions so they become second nature. It is only through these steps that we can understand and create the lives we desire. We are already doing most of these steps unconsciously, which is why we are alive and functioning. The goal of this book is to get you to wake up to the knowledge that we have control over our lives. We must learn to see the world and our place in it, and take responsibility for where our lives are. It is through this responsibility that we will learn to take back our power and create our lives.

If you wake up every morning and have negative thoughts, you are practicing to be negative. Through repetition, we master the ideas and actions that drive our lives. This is how we learn and shape our lives into what they are. People who are negative all the time are often totally unaware of how negative they have become.

It becomes second nature to them because they have practiced and mastered the skill of seeing the world in a negative light. It is with great ease that they can see the negative in any positive situation. We see these people and often wonder, "Why is that person so negative?" Little do we know that by asking that question, we are practicing being judgmental.

We see the actions in another and judge them as good or bad, right or wrong. This is also a practice that forms our lives. We practice judging others by judging ourselves. We often feel we are not good enough, not smart enough, not lucky enough, and not worthy enough for love or happiness in our lives. By repeating this pattern of thought, we develop the skill of self-doubt. Some people become such masters of self-doubt that they become unaware that they no longer even try to better themselves. They immediately convince themselves they cannot achieve something, so they don't even entertain the idea of attempting it. Through repetition, we can become the biggest success or the most colossal failure we work to become. All that is required is repetition and intention.

Look at professional athletes. They train their bodies and minds to such a high level that others in the world cannot accomplish the same skills. It's not because others lack the potential physical abilities to do the activity, but they have not committed the same amount of time to developing the skills necessary to achieve success at that level. It is true that most athletes are born with physical attributes that allow them to excel with ease in the beginning, but very few reach an elite level on physical skill alone. It is only through practice and mastering the skills required do they reach their full potential.

We are all born with infinite potential. Through practice, we can master the skills we desire. If we do this with intention, we can focus this ability and create what we want. Good eating habits, a healthy lifestyle, positive thinking, being relaxed – all of these things can be learned and improved through practice. In fact, they cannot be learned or improved any other way. It is not possible to learn to do something without trying it over and over again. Some people may learn the first time, but only through repetition will that skill improve and become more mastered.

It is also important to note that no other person can teach you anything. Only you can choose to learn what is being shown, and that learning can only happen through practice. No other person can teach you lessons; they can only put the information in front of you. You can either practice to retain that information and apply it as part of your being or practice to put it aside and forget it. Practicing to put it aside is much easier to do, so often this is what people choose. This choice also becomes a habit, making it harder and harder to retain information. When they are introduced to something they may want to retain and use, they often find this difficult because they've developed the skill to push information aside rather than absorbing it and putting it to good use.

A good illustration of this is seen in people who use hypnosis to stop bad habits like smoking. Some people use hypnosis to place a suggestion into their subconscious, telling themselves they no longer want to smoke. The normal reaction to this is that, upon awakening from the hypnotic state, the person does not want to smoke. This is only a temporary state, however. If this person continues the practice of not smoking, they will successfully stop smoking. Others will not practice non-smoking and eventually fall back into the habit of smoking. These people will say, "That didn't work." In reality, the hypnosis was a starting point to help direct them but the practice of their actions after that decided if this would be successful or not. When we understand how to direct our practice, we can use it to achieve anything in life that we desire.

When we practice without intention, or subconsciously, we blindly go about creating skills that often we don't want in our lives. We don't want to judge people or be critical. We don't want to be negative or always expect the worst from the world, but often that's how people are. They have spent the better part of their years practicing to be this way. They repeat bad habits in their lives and aren't even aware that they are mastering skills they don't want.

In order to change these skills, we must practice new skills with intention. We can't force ourselves to unlearn ideas through practice, the same way we learned them. But by learning new skills in their place, the old ones will simply fade away over time from lack of use.

In neuroscience, which is the scientific study of the brain, this act is called "synaptic pruning." It is the process of removing connections between neurons in the brain that are no longer used.

There is a phrase used in neuroscience that says "neurons that fire together, wire together." This essentially means that when you experience something, like feeling fear in a public place, the neurons in your brain connect the experience of feeling fear with the experience of being in a public place. This means the next time you are in a public place, the feeling of fear will arise in you with much greater ease because a neural connection has been made. The more times you experience being in public and feeling fearful, the stronger that connection becomes. Essentially, you are practicing feeling fear. This neural wiring that happens is what eventually turns our conscious fearful thoughts into subconscious fears that appear seemingly out of nowhere. We've just practiced being afraid so much that the brain takes over and reacts for us.

When we start any new way of being, it will seem very foreign to us. Just like anything else we learn, it may seem forced or challenging at the start. This is natural because we are not used to doing what it is we have started to practice. Our mind and our body will have a natural response already learned and in place that it will try use as a response. After all, you've been practicing to react a certain way for months or even years. You can't just shut that reaction off overnight.

So, staying committed to your new practice is critical. more one practices something, the easier it gets. Keeping the intention of why you want to learn this new skill is necessary to keep the practice focused in the correct direction. Remember, even quitting is a practiced skill. When things get hard, if one constantly gives up, that person is practicing giving up when things get hard. If we persevere through those tough moments, we are practicing to stay strong and committed to what it is we desire. When that is practiced, the skill of perseverance will become easier.

When using techniques like meditation or mindfulness, it's important to allow patience for yourself to develop these skills. Mastering them will take time, just like everything else you've ever learned. Every skill you know took time to learn and master. Crying, rolling over, crawling, walking, talking, feeding yourself, using the bathroom, reading, writing, riding a bike, driving a car, operating a computer – everything you can do today had to be learned over time. You will learn to do new skills this same way.

Once a practice is selected, it is important to allow your heart and feeling to be a major part of the process of practicing. It is not enough to simply "go through the motions" when you practice. This will help you to learn what you need, but it will not help you to "be" what you need to be. The heart and feelings are major players in the process when it comes to what we call spiritual practices or matters of the soul. It helps you to "be" the practice, rather than just doing the practice. This is very important.

How many times have you tried to do or learn something and you kept repeating to yourself, "I'm never going to get this!"? How many times were you successful at getting it? Probably not very often. This is because you didn't align your emotional state with your intellectual state. Getting your physical actions on the same page as your emotional ones is critical to putting you on the fast track to learning and growing.

The heart is the emotional center of our body. The heart and mind are constantly sending signals back and forth regarding the body's emotional state, much like a two-way radio. The heart actually transmits more information to the brain than the brain does to the heart regarding emotional states. This is why the old adage "fake it until you make it" isn't always the best advice. In truth, if your mind is telling you one thing but your heart is telling you another, the heart will win out over the brain.

This is why feeling a strong and empowered emotional state is so critical to successfully developing a new habit, because if you don't believe it, you can't achieve it. You must know in your heart that you can do this first. If you just go through the motions without really believing that you can accomplish what it is you are trying to do, you will never fully commit and therefore never fully master the skill.

How you feel is the language of the heart. When you feel inspired, happy, peaceful, grateful, appreciative, and positive, the heart communicates that to the brain and to the rest of the universe. I can tell you from personal experience that what you put out to the universe in the form of energy is also returned to you. This means, when you are a negative person putting out negative energy, you will receive negative energy back to you in the form of people, actions, and events. But when you put out peaceful, calm, and loving energy, you will also receive that back. Now this doesn't mean that only bad things happen to bad people and good things happen to good people. Nor does it mean that we deserve the bad things that happen to us. That can be a very dangerous and self-destructive way of seeing the world, especially for people who have suffered through real trauma in their life. It isn't a question of victim blaming but rather recognizing that the world is full of energy, both positive and negative. When you put out more positive energy, you increase your chances for having more positive energy return.

So while you are working on consciously developing new habits, do not focus your attention on *not* having the skill in which you are practicing! By doing this, you will actually make it more difficult to attain the new ability. This is because your energy is putting out the idea of you *not* having the skill or the feeling of lacking what you desire. When you put forth energy of lacking, you will attract more lacking! But if you can feel yourself learning and growing in a positive way, you will learn and grow faster and with much greater ease.

When you practice anything, make sure you are focused on being positive. Smile often as you practice. If something is a challenge that day, do not judge the challenge, simply accept it for what it is and continue moving forward with the understanding that it is helping you to learn and grow.

So how do we use the idea of practicing with intention to actually change things in our lives? For me, it came in the form of four steps I like to call "changing with E.A.S.E." – education, awareness, strategy, and execution.

Step One: Education

In order to learn how to do something, you must first understand what needs to go into what you want to do. Learning the ins and outs of basic principles behind a skill is critical to understanding how to master it.

In the past, when people wanted to learn a new skill or trade, they would become an apprentice to someone who had already mastered the skills we desired to learn. Today, it's a little easier to access knowledge or education but that does not mean the skills will not take the same effort and commitment to learn.

If you want to develop skills in life, you'll want to learn from those who have done them and are already successful. Education is the key to changing your life. I don't mean simply getting as many degrees as you can. To me, there is a difference between getting a degree and getting an education. A degree proves to the world that you've done the coursework required to master a trade or to do a job with proficiency. I know many people who have spent thousands of dollars getting their degree but didn't fully learn how to do the job they wanted until they received practical training in the field.

In today's high-tech world, education is all around us. You can read books, watch videos, attend events and workshops, and even take classes online to learn how to do just about anything. From meditation to welding, the internet has become a very useful tool for sharing and teaching how to do just about anything.

So the first step is to learn as much as you can about what it is you are trying to develop as a skill. In fact, you should never stop learning! I read as much as I can on as many topics as I can. Learning about a variety of topics – such as neuroscience, meditation, Buddhism, Christianity, Hinduism, diet, exercise, breathing, psychology, philosophy, entrepreneurship, business, writing, marketing, and spirituality – has made it possible for me to control and overcome my issues with anxiety and panic disorders in my own life, and how I've learned to share my story with others. I now have a passion for learning because each time I do, I give myself an opportunity to improve my life and the lives of those around me.

Education can change everything, so never stop learning.

Step Two: Awareness

Learning to become self-aware is one of the most underutilized tools that we have at our disposal. You can't know what it is you are doing wrong until you take a long, hard look at what it is you are doing first. This is very challenging for most people because we all fear failure on some level. No one likes to admit when they are wrong or that they are not doing something correctly.

I'm here to tell you, if your fear of failure is keeping you from taking a look at yourself, your past, your thoughts, your emotions, or your actions, please know that everyone fails at something in his or her life. Failure is almost required in order to build something that has never been built, learn something you didn't know, or discover something no one else has ever discovered.

Need proof? Here's a short list of some of the world's most successful people who failed in dramatic fashion before they ever found success:

- **Walt Disney** was told he lacked creativity when he was fired from his newspaper job.

- **Steve Jobs** created Apple, one of the largest computer empires ever, only to be fired by the company's board of directors.
- **Bill Gates**' first company was called Traf-O-Data and was designed to process and analyze traffic tape data. The product didn't work and the company failed, unlike his next venture, Microsoft.
- **Henry Ford** failed all his early business attempts and was left broke five times before he founded Ford Motor Company.
- **Thomas Edison** was once told by his teacher that he was "too stupid to learn anything." He had over a thousand failed attempts before successfully inventing the light bulb.
- **Oprah Winfrey**, one of the most iconic people on television, was fired from her job as a television reporter because she was "unfit for TV."
- Theodor Seuss Geisel, better know as **Dr. Seuss**, had his first book, *To Think That I Saw It on Mulberry Street*, rejected by twenty-seven publishers.
- **Steven Spielberg**, one of the world's most celebrated film directors, was rejected by the University of Southern California School of Theater, Film, and Television three times before eventually enrolling at another school. He dropped out and began directing before returning thirty-five years later to complete his work and earn his bachelor's degree.
- **Stephen King** had his first book, *Carrie*, rejected by thirty publishers before he gave up and threw it in the trash. His wife removed it from the trash and encouraged him to keep trying. He is now one of the best-selling authors of all time.
- **Michael Jordan**, arguably one of the greatest basketball players ever, was actually cut from his high school

basketball team. He has famously stated, "I have missed more than 9,000 shots in my career. I have lost almost 300 games. On 26 occasions, I have been entrusted to take the game-winning shot, and I missed. I have failed over and over and over again in my life. And that is why I succeed."

So it's time to put failure into perspective. In many ways, it is absolutely necessary in order to succeed. If you don't fail, you are not challenging yourself enough. Failing isn't bad, it's just a single step toward an ultimate goal. Failure is a temporary state, but it is not who you are.

Learning to look at your success and failure with a healthy distance between you and the actions is key to not taking failure so personally. You are not success and you are not failure. You are simply the person taking the action that is later defined as one or the other based on how it is compared to similar actions and results.

If you really want to become better at anything, you need to learn to see your actions with a healthy understanding that what you've done does not dictate all that you can ever be. We all make mistakes. We all fail. We all do the wrong thing from time to time. It's how we learn and grow as people. If you are not failing, you are not pushing yourself or challenging yourself enough, and you are definitely not growing.

But how does someone become more self-aware? It isn't exactly easy to do, which is why so few people are able to do it. The biggest challenge to being self-aware is that you are often far too close to yourself to see things from the proper perspective. Often, you are so invested in your own perspective, your own beliefs, and your own reality that you can't honestly see what you are doing wrong because you believe everything you are doing is right. Why else would you be doing it?

Sure, many of us say things like, "Everything I do is wrong," but how many people actually believe that to be true? If you really believed it was wrong, you wouldn't keep making those same choices. But even when you intellectually know something is wrong, often it feels right at the time. I'm here to tell you that just because something feels right doesn't mean it is in your best interest to do it.

Many times we find ourselves making the same bad choices because we've become stuck in a rut that we call "our life." It feels good because it is familiar to us. We understand it and can relate to it because we have become used to what it feels like. But it is amazing how many awful things we can become used to feeling.

In order to break out of this slump of doing things just because they feel right at the time, you need to add a little perspective to your life. You need to put some emotional distance between yourself and your choices, and then look at them from this new vantage point. It's sort of like looking at something through a microscope. Sometimes you are too close to see what something is until you pull back and change how close you are. When you give yourself distance, you have a chance to see the bigger picture. What something looks like up close will look very different once there is some distance.

The other challenge is determining what you need to become aware of. Most of the big choices are easy to see. We know when a choice requires us to sit back and deliberate over what actions are best for us to take. Often, people create pros and cons lists that allow them to see all the reasons they should do something on one side of a piece of paper and all the reasons they shouldn't do something on the other side. This allows you to add up both lists, compare them, and make an educated decision as to what choice you should make.

But what about all the other little choices you are faced with on an almost-constant basis every day? Would you ever consider making a pros and cons list for deciding to feel annoyed that it was raining outside when you woke up, and if you should feel negative or positive about that? Probably not. Something like being annoyed about the weather just feels like an obvious reaction to a situation.

It's raining and everyone feels crappy when it's raining out, right?

That reaction is exactly the type of choice that seems really small but actually has a tremendous impact on you.

Your life is made up of small daily actions. The accumulation of these actions becomes the hours, the days, the weeks, the months, and the years of your life. The biggest challenge is most people don't connect their daily actions with the outcome of their life. They look at their life and wonder why they are not where they want to be, yet they never take the step to connect their daily actions to where they ended up.

It's like getting into a car and driving west and then complaining that you are not heading east. If getting directions is education, then recognizing which direction you've been driving is awareness. Too many people complain about their life, as if someone else has been in control. You are in control of your own life. You can choose to take action, or you can choose to let your subconscious mind take action for you.

Most people live in a state of subconsciousness, wandering through life while on autopilot, always complaining they never get where they really want to go. Becoming aware that your everyday actions dictate the outcome of your life puts your hands back on the wheel and gives you back control of the direction of your life.

The way you do this is to start to look at how your daily actions support or undermine what it is you really want out of life. If you want to get into better shape, then sitting on the couch, watching television, and eating a bag of chips isn't going to make it happen. If you didn't know that, the education part of the process will tell you that. But once you know what you should and shouldn't eat, it becomes your responsibility to take the right actions that support the desired outcome.

But there is a downside to becoming self-aware that you should know about. Once you commit to becoming aware of the things you do, you will no longer be able to claim ignorance to the fact that you are doing them. Some people are blissfully ignorant to how they act. There is actually a name for this, called the Dunning-Kruger effect. This is when someone is truly unable to accurately determine his or her own competency level, or incompetency level to be more exact. In other words, it's when a person is too ignorant to know he is ignorant.

Or to quote the Chinese philosophical writings of the Tao Te Ching, "Those who think they know never learn."

So if you are okay with giving up the plausible deniability of not knowing why your life is out of control, becoming more self-aware will allow you to see what it is you are doing and what impact those actions are having on your life.

Step Three: Strategy

The third step to changing your habits is to put a strategy in place that will help you take new actions. This will put you in a better position to achieve what you want in life. Which strategy you employ greatly depends on what habits you try to develop. The secret to this step isn't in your ability to find the correct strategy, but in your willingness to follow through with whatever strategy you decide to pursue.

In today's day and age, strategies are everywhere. Anything you want to learn how to do, there are hundreds of books, recordings, videos, and classes available to you. There are books on changing your spending habits, your eating habits, your sleeping habits, your thinking habits, and your diet and exercise habits; you name something, and a quick Google search will lead you to more resources than you'll know what to do with.

Even this very book has strategies on how to be more mindful, improve how you speak to yourself, lower stress and anxiety through meditation, and many other tips and tools anyone can use to change how their brain reacts to the outside, and inside, world we live in. But like I said at the beginning of this book, a strategy is only as good as the fourth step in this process.

Step Four: Execution

The difference between people who are successful in life and those who feel as if life has left them behind can usually be determined by looking at the amount of effort and execution to put into anything they want to do. I know this firsthand because I'm guilty of poor execution when it comes to following through on what I wanted to do for most of my life.

Over the years, I've purchased many books, just like the one you're reading right now. I've read them cover to cover. I highlighted lines that stood out to me as meaningful or aha moments. I've written notes in the margins. I've even sung the books' praises to friends and family telling them that they should read the book.

But for many years, once the initial energy, inspiration, and spike of dopamine faded from this new idea I had just learned, rather than taking it and putting it into action, I simply looked for another book that would give me that same excited feeling. I'd find another teacher that promised to show me how to fix my life, change my mind-set, or ease my pain. They all gave me different advice, each more exciting than the next. But none of them ever told me the most important part. Maybe it was implied in what they had written. Maybe most rational people assumed it would be the logical step in the process and it didn't need to be spelled out to the reader. But it was something that was lost on me, and I want to make sure it isn't lost on you. It's why I started this book with it and why I'm repeating it here.

The problem with this pattern is that I never executed any of the strategies that were written on the pages of all those great books. I never took action and implemented those ideas into my day-to-day life. I didn't make those processes part of who I was and what I did. Because I never executed those strategies, I never created the results they promised. I never changed my life, because you don't change your life by reading a book or by being exposed to an idea. You change your life by altering the things you do while you are living that life. You do something different than what you did before. You add a new element that wasn't there before. And then, over time, your life becomes different, because the sum of the actions you've taken are different.

Your life is the sum of your actions. It isn't stagnant or fixed, but moving and changing with each breath. Every second of every day, you have an opportunity to make a new choice, walk down a new path, or strengthen your resolve to follow the road you are already on. Knowing which choice is correct and which is folly is heavily dependent upon the first three steps, but those steps are useless without the fourth step – execution.

If you are anything like me – and since you are reading this book, there is a good chance that you are – your anxiety and fear have kept you from taking the necessary steps to execute the right strategies in your life. Maybe you're worried you haven't found the strategy. Maybe you're unsure if this path is the right one for you. Maybe you just can't move forward without having a guarantee that it will work or that you won't fail. This is where it becomes critical for you to know what your motivation for change is. This is when your why becomes the driving force behind finally taking action or simply thinking about it.

If you didn't complete the questions from Chapter 2, I'd suggest going back and revisiting that section. Figure out exactly what your why is and create your reminder image that you keep in plain sight. This is important because it will help keep you on the path to actually executing on the other three steps listed here.

It will take effort, time, and commitment: You'll need to work to educate yourself on what you want to change. You must become aware of what daily actions you are taking that do not support the changes you are trying to make in your life. You'll want to find a strategy that will work for you. And then, finally, you must execute on that strategy.

No matter how dedicated you are or how strong-willed a person you can be, even the most driven people have times when they want to throw in the towel, curl up on the couch, and give in to what feels easy, comfortable, and safe. Those are the moments when you need to sit and look at your "why" image and remember. Allow those feelings and emotions to well up within you, giving you the determination to keep going.

Changing your life isn't easy. It takes work. There is no quick fix or easy solution. Anyone who tells you otherwise is trying to sell you something. Even when you have all the tools and understanding, life has a way of challenging you and testing your resolve.

But when you finally begin to wake up to the truth of who you are and what you are capable of accomplishing – and just how simple the process can be – life becomes a game that can be enjoyed rather than suffered through. There are so many wonderful things you can create and experience. All you need to do is open your heart, mind, and soul to the idea that, with all your failures and all your limitations, the only failures are the things you don't try, and the only limitations are the ones you place on dreams.

"I learned that courage was not the absence of fear, but the triumph over it. The brave man is not he who does not feel afraid, but he who conquers that fear."
– Nelson Mandela

CHAPTER 10: FEAR VS. DANGER

I stood looking up into the edge of the darkness, with no idea what was waiting for me at the top. Frozen with fear, my mind raced with thoughts that made the tiny hairs on my arms stand on end. The stairs before us ascended into nothingness—a black empty cavern, devoid of life, waiting for someone to enter.

What was lying in wait? Something horrible, for certain, of this I was sure. I knew for sure that before I got to the top step, something hideous would reach down and snatch me up before I could even scream.

"Go on," said my brother, standing directly behind me.

Terror surged through my body, and I frantically thought of any excuse to avoid entering that abyss and whatever horrors it contained. In an instant, I was struck by inspiration.

"Water!" I yelled at last. "I need a drink of water."

I quickly turned and rushed past my bewildered brother, almost taking him down with me. With an annoyed huff, he used his much larger body to push me back, which sent me crashing into the wall.

I struggled to keep my balance as I felt my feet slip out from under me. The limited traction offered by my sock-covered feet offered little resistance against the smooth carpeting at the base of our stairs. I regained my composure and entered the kitchen for my drink. A sense of relief settled in as I heard the familiar click of the light switch from the top of the stairs.

My brother, in turning on our bedroom light, had obviously sent whatever was hiding in the darkness scurrying for cover. I had successfully avoided stepping into that dark, ominous room once more. I finished my water and safely went up to bed.

While this might sound a bit dramatic for a five-year-old who was afraid of the dark, stepping into our bedroom with no lights on was just as terrifying an experience for me as anything anyone else might experience. Our bedroom was a converted attic-space in where the light switch was most unfortunately located at the top of the stairs instead of the bottom. This required us to walk all the way up the dark stairs and step into the room before being able to turn on the light. This act terrified me every night. Not because there had ever been anything waiting for me when I went up, but because I thought there might be. My fear became real because my mind made it real.

I never asked my brother to go first and turn on the light. I didn't want to tell him I was scared. I figured he would make fun of me for being a baby, tell all our friends I was afraid of the dark, and then everyone else would make fun of me. In fact, I never told anyone this.

I would fight with him about not going up to our room first. I'd make up excuses to stay downstairs until after he went up. I'd start going upstairs first and then pretend I forgot something and go down again. I did all these things, but I never simply said, "Pat, I'm afraid of the dark. Will you go up and turn on the light for me?"

I never said this because I was afraid of two things: the fear of the unknown and the fear of being singled out and judged because of my fear. Two fears I would battle my entire life.

But that fear I felt as a child had nothing to do with what was actually there. My room was still my room. I knew exactly what was there; the toys, clothes, and furniture were all the same during daylight hours as they were in the dark. I probably could have walked around in that room with my eyes shut and not even bumped into anything. But remove the light, and suddenly my room became filled with the most terrifying creatures imaginable. On some level, I knew this wasn't true. But without the light illuminating the truth, I couldn't be one hundred percent sure.

There was always something innately scary to me about not knowing exactly what was ahead of me.

In many ways, this was the beginning of what would eventually evolve into my anxiety disorder and become the source of my panic attacks. The "not knowing" left space for my mind to wander. And because of how I had been taught to think, it always wandered into the negative. Most of my experiences told me something bad was going to happen and that I needed to fear the unknown. A combination of expecting something bad to happen and not knowing always caused me to assume the worst.

It was as if I lived my entire life like choices were dark rooms. I couldn't see what was ahead of me, so I assumed something bad was lurking in the darkness. And because I was afraid I'd be judged for my fear, I didn't dare tell anyone I was afraid.

Everywhere I looked, every opportunity that presented itself, and every person I came in contact with were all situations that could go wrong.

I spent my childhood afraid of the dark, and now, because of my negative outlook and thinking, I was living my adult life in the dark as well. I was afraid of what I could not clearly see, so I imagined everything that I saw was a threat, hiding behind the next turn.

Much like having my brother turn on the light first, I believed that maybe if I saw it coming early enough I could do something to prevent it from happening. I could avoid the negative outcome if I could see it coming.

Many of the people I've talked to about anxiety feel this way. We convince ourselves that by always looking for the problem, we prepare ourselves better to deal with it when it inevitably arrives.

When we do this, we give our anxiety a value it does not deserve. We see it as useful and necessary. If we are not expecting the worst, we will be surprised and caught unprepared by what happens. It would be our own fault because we were not ready to deal with the situation, so we must always be on guard.

Anxiety becomes our default setting, and we refuse to change that setting because we believe it serves us. We believe our hypervigilance keeps us safe and protected from what might be waiting for us in the darkness of our own expectations. If it didn't go badly this time, just wait – it will probably go wrong next time and I have a responsibility to myself to be ready. It would be irresponsible for me to not be prepared, to relax, or to let down my guard. It would only take a second for something bad to happen, so if I'm not prepared every second of every day, expecting the unexpected, I would be responsible for whatever bad thing happened. It would be my fault, so that would mean I would deserve it. I wasn't able to prevent it, so it must be my fault. It's my fault if something happened to me. It's my fault if something happened to a loved one. It's my fault if something happened to anyone. The only way to stop it from happening is to expect the unexpected. The only way to feel safe is to never let down your guard, to never feel safe.

Now, for most people, this may seem like an extreme exaggeration. And for most people, it is. But for people who struggle with anxiety, it is an all-too-common state of being. Even people who do not suffer from some form of diagnosable anxiety disorder can probably still relate on some level to this feeling. After all, fear isn't exclusive to those of us who struggle with a anxiety.

And to be clear, fear isn't always a bad thing. Being prepared for things that could happen is often necessary and can be critical for survival. In many ways, we do things all the time that keep us safe. The choices we make are often derived by our desire to have no harm happen to us. It isn't abnormal to want to be safe. But when you see every situation as a life-or-death struggle, stress levels can rise and remain at unhealthy levels.

We have to learn to understand that there is a true difference between fear and danger. And understanding this difference becomes a critical component to managing our fear and learning to live our lives in a way that excites us, challenges us, and allows us to pursue our dreams, whether that dream is to start a business, write a book, try a sport, or simply leave our house.

Now, I want to be very clear about something: Fear is not real, but danger is.

The reason this is important to understand is because the best way to overcome your fear is to face it. But knowing the difference between fear and danger could be the difference between you overcoming your anxiety and ending up in the emergency room.

I never want anyone to ever do something that is going to cause physical harm or injury to himself or herself, or to any other person or animal. Overcoming anxiety is not about controlling or changing others. It is about learning to stand up and face the feeling that is created deep within yourself.

Worry and fear are good in the face of real danger.

Often when faced with a dangerous situation, our body reacts in a way that greatly increases our chances of survival, especially when confronted by a life-or-death situation. But how often are the situations we worry about actually dangerous? It's far less often then our minds would make us believe.

For most people with anxiety, almost every situation feels like life or death. That is the root of our problem. Our mind causes our body to react to a situation with an increased threat level when the danger is only created in our minds, not in our environments.

Being afraid of something that poses a true physical harm to you is a good thing. Our goal is not to become people who blindly tempt fate and put ourselves in a dangerous situation all in the name of facing our fears.

If you have a fear of bears, by no means should you face that fear by going to your local zoo, climbing into the bear cage, and confronting your fear head on. If you do, there is a good chance you will not survive. The danger you'd put yourself in would be real, and the fear of that bear mauling you would be completely justified.

But if you have an irrational fear of bears that causes you to never leave the house or go for walks outside, facing your fears would have more to do with understanding that the threat of a bear attacking you as you walk down the street is slim. Learning to deal with the physical anxiety of walking outside is what you need to confront – not the actual bear.

I say this because it is important to understand that fear is not real. Fear is a reaction in our mind, not a physical thing we can hold. This doesn't mean that the feeling of fear doesn't exist. It absolutely does. We all know that feeling afraid is a real feeling. But the physical, imminent threat that the fear is preparing you for oftentimes is not real.

But danger is real. If you are in a dangerous situation, feeling fear and worry is natural, understandable, and useful. Fear and anxiety sharpen your mind's focus on danger and prepare your body for a fight, flight, or freeze response. That is the primitive part of our physical nature.

When we lived in the wild, if confronted by a wild animal, our body would physically prepare itself to either fight the animal head on, run away quickly, or freeze in place, whichever option gave us the greatest chance of survival.

That is why when we become nervous, our hearts race, our palms and foreheads get sweaty, and we feel like we are on sensory overload. Our heart is busy pumping extra blood to the muscles in our body so they have enough oxygen to work harder and faster if needed. Our bodies also shut down the functions of other less-critical internal organs so they can divert needed resources to power parts of the body that are critical to survival.

This is why stress can be so damaging to our bodies over time. When we are always in a state of fight, flight, or freeze, we cause our inner body to become overworked, and it will eventually break down. For someone who never exercises or eats right, suddenly taxing his or her heart with an overload of work can be dangerous.

But the number of times in our lives that we actually find ourselves in a dangerous situation is often very few compared to the number of times our mind tells our body that we are in danger. When you suffer from anxiety, you are almost always in a state of fear, and your body is always being asked to stay in a state of high alert. Our goal is to understand why our mind is doing this, to overcome that irrational fear of a danger that is not present, and to learn to calm the mind and body so we don't feel anxious all the time.

For many people who have suffered from anxiety for long periods of time, the pattern of fear has become imprinted in the mind. That pattern needs to be faced and overcome in order to rewire the brain to react differently to the situation. We need to create a new habit of how we react so our minds can have a new default response to situations that often cause us to feel uneasy or uncomfortable.

Things often trigger an anxious reaction. That trigger can be reprogrammed in our mind so our reaction isn't one of anxiety but one of something more beneficial to us.

When you have a fear of public speaking, like I do, the idea of standing in front of people makes your mind react in a way that tells the body it is in danger. The first thing you do is to begin visualizing yourself standing on a stage as the fear engulfs you. Even if you are nowhere near a stage, your brain creates a picture so clear that your body doesn't know the difference between what is real and what is only in your mind. Visualization is a very powerful tool. Most people use it all the time and are not even aware they are using it.

In fact, that is a common theme for people throughout their lives. Everything we do is some form of a pattern. It is a repetition of actions repeated until it becomes part of our subconscious mind. This entire book is a collection of patterns that you are most likely already implementing in your daily lives, you are just doing it subconsciously. When you become more aware of your actions and your emotions, you'll begin to interrupt those patterns when they start. This will allow you to also become more intentional with these patterns and use these skills to consciously build your life, rather than subconsciously or in many cases unconsciously build your life.

Visualization is a great way to be able to practice doing things without actually doing them. This is the first step in learning how to face your fears in a safe and controlled way.

You already know how powerful this can be. In fact, you already use it, you are just unaware that you do.

Most of us use it so often that we are completely unaware it's what we are doing. In fact, I would argue that any fear you have is simply your mind visualizing an outcome that you don't want and then responding as if it is actually happening. We have the ability to get so detailed in our thoughts that our body begins to physically respond to what is going on, even though it is only created in our mind.

There is some real-world science that backs up this reality.

A Harvard neuroscientist named Alvaro Pascual-Leone conducted an experiment designed to study the brain activity in subjects learning a five-finger piano exercise. The volunteers were asked to practice for two hours a day for five days and had their brain activity mapped using what is called a transcranial-magnetic-stimulation (TMS) test before and after each practice session. In both groups, the TMS data showed expansion in the motor cortex region of the brain responsible for the finger movement. Once the group had shown proficiency in the exercise, they were split into two groups. One group continued to practice for another four weeks, while the second group stopped practicing altogether. As expected, the group with additional practice time showed continued brain activity and expansion while the group that stopped practicing returned to its original baseline mapping.

The amazing part of the experiment came when the study expanded to include a group that simply visualized the five-finger piano exercise without physically playing the exercise on the piano. When they compared the TMS data, they saw the same expansion in the motor cortex regions of the brains of those who only visualized playing but never actually touched the piano.

This means that the brain couldn't tell the difference between actually doing the activity or simply thinking about doing the activity. It actively and physically changed itself as if had played the piano.

So why is this so important when it comes to anxiety? Because when we spend all our time visualizing the worst-case scenarios, we are actually rewiring our minds as if these things are actually happening. Our mind doesn't know the difference between what we are physically experiencing and what we imagine we are experiencing. This is why our reactions to our fearful thoughts become so real to us. Our mind doesn't know the difference between what's happening in our mind and what's going on in the real world. It is then possible to begin to fear something that's never actually happened before. That process of mentally putting ourselves in what we perceive to be dangerous situations causes our minds to rewire as if those situations actually were dangerous. This pattern causes our brain to wire itself in such a way that we fear things we've never experienced because our minds believe we have.

Here's an example: One evening, I was home sitting on my couch watching television. It was a sitcom that I had seen hundreds of times before. For some reason, I began to think about what it would be like to be an actor on a sitcom. I began to imagine that I was actually on the set of the show. I pictured myself delivering my lines and what it would feel like filming in front of a live studio audience. I could see the set and the lights, the cameras and the crew, and even the audience.

I saw myself sitting on the couch with my fellow actors sitting on either side of me. I could feel the heat of the lights on my skin. I could see the eyes of the audience focused on my every move. I could imagine the pressure of having to remember my lines and deliver them flawlessly. I began to worry about what could go wrong.

What if I forgot what I was supposed to say?
What if I got nervous and began to sweat?
What if the audience saw me start to panic?
What if I felt the urge to get up and leave, but we were in the middle of a scene with all the other actors?

Suddenly, my heart started racing. My chest tightened. I felt hot all over and began sweating. I started to panic and couldn't breathe. I was having a panic attack sitting on my own couch, mentally surrounded by all those actors, the entire audience, and the crew of the show.

In reality, I wasn't anywhere near a sitcom stage. There were no actors around me, nor any cameras or audience watching me. None of that was real. It was only happening in my mind. But it felt real. It felt so real that my body reacted as if it were actually happening to me at that moment.

I remember clearly getting upset with myself, realizing that I was having a panic attack sitting at home on my couch. What was wrong with me? Why couldn't I even feel safe in my own home?

The combination of my anxious, negative thinking and my overactive imagination created a scenario in my mind where I believed I was in danger and my body reacted. After this happened, I began subconsciously repeating the visualization of being an actor on a show, and over time started to have more panic attacks while watching television. Every time I'd watch a show, I'd picture myself as part of the cast. The sensations would immediately return and cause me to feel anxious.

The pattern of experiencing something – attaching anxiety or panic to that situation and then allowing my body to react as if I were in danger – continued to get stronger and stronger. Each time this happened, I was practicing to be afraid. I was experiencing fear without any real danger being present. But my mind didn't understand that because I had rewired it to believe there was danger. That is what most of us do in our lives every day.

We fear things as if they are dangerous, even when there is no real danger to be had. The things we find dangerous today are far more ego based rather than survival based. We see danger in losing money, being rejected, not being loved, not being successful, failing at something, or having someone think poorly of us. None of these things are really dangerous directly. Sure, without money you won't be able to buy food or provide shelter for yourself. But how many of us are actually on the brink of starvation at the point we fear losing money? Most of that fear comes from visualizing into the future of what our life would be like if we lost money and went a significant amount of time without it. We project a possible future scenario onto our current situation, causing us to fear something that isn't even happening.

This is what is meant by the saying "A coward dies a thousand deaths." When you are afraid of dying, you imagine what it's like to experience that death happening over and over again. Even though it would be something you'd only experience once, speaking specifically in the case of death, when you live your life in fear, your mind practices it and rewires your mind to become accustomed to that experience. To your mind, you have died a thousand deaths.

So what can we do about this? How do we go about understanding the difference between fear and danger? And more importantly, how can we learn to use the functionality of our mind in a way that helps us rather than limits our potential?

Any time I am feeling fearful, I have four questions I ask myself.
1. Am I in physical danger?
2. How does this fear serve me?
3. What is the best-case scenario?
4. Can I face this fear?

Each question has a specific purpose that will help you deal with the immediate, short-term situation you are faced with at the time. But there is also a more permanent, long-term benefit to this line of questioning that will help you overcome your anxiety moving forward. This is the simple fact that by asking yourself questions you are breaking the pattern of how your brain processes anxiety. This interruption of the habitual thought pattern is part of a process I like to call the alphabet approach to changing your subconscious mind. I'll cover process this in greater detail in chapter 12 so for now we'll simply focus on the questions.

Question One: Am I in Physical Danger?

This is the first question you should ask yourself, because it is the most important when it comes to how fearful you need to be in any given situation. Oftentimes, fear can be a good indicator that you are putting yourself in a stressful or challenging situation. But just because something is challenging doesn't necessarily mean you are in real, physical danger.

Since the body doesn't really know how to distinguish between fear and danger, you need to mentally take control and open a direct line of communication with yourself. This is done simply by consciously talking to yourself, taking stock of what is really going on around you, and rationally and calmly assessing the true situation.

Look around you and ask yourself if you are in true, physical danger. Is it a dangerous situation that threatens your personal safety? Are you in a situation where another person could do you physical harm? Are you putting yourself at an unnecessary risk? What are the chances that if things go wrong that you would suffer a physical injury?

Some things we do are physically dangerous. Skydiving, hang gliding, cliff jumping, rock climbing and bungee jumping are examples of dangerous or high-risk activities that some people choose to participate in. These people – "adrenaline junkies" – tend to seek the adrenaline rush that occurs when the body is placed in a dangerous and physically demanding scenario. They say that it makes them feel alive and energized. They desire the high that is created when they tempt fate or cheat death.

Other people may look at flying in a plane, driving a car, or even going out in public as things that spike their adrenaline and cause them to experience that fearful emotion. While there is some inherent danger in almost everything we do, the level of danger presented in flying in a plane compared to jumping out of one are not quite the same. What makes the difference is the percentage of risk involved in both activities.

There is some form of risk involved in everything we do. That risk can be minimized by the actions we take. It is possible that you could be hit by a bus while crossing the street in a busy city, but the risk of that happening is greatly reduced if you stop and look both ways rather than just blindly stepping off the curb and into traffic. This is how fear can be a good thing. It reminds you that you must take some precautions to ensure your safety. But when that fear gets out of control, we tend to take overly drastic measures to reduce the risk of injury or harm. You can lessen the risk of being hit by a bus to almost zero by never going into the city or never crossing the street when you are there, but both of these activities will severely impact your ability to enjoy life and do things you may be required to do. The idea is to understand the true level of risk associated with real danger and mitigate that risk alone, rather than trying to avoid every possible situation that poses any risk, regardless how small.

Question Two: How Does This Fear Serve Me?

In almost every scenario, our fear serves some sort of purpose. Exactly what that purpose might be can be challenging to fully understand, especially if we are not truthful regarding why we are afraid.

In situations of actual danger, the feeling of fear helps sharpen our senses and better prepare ourself for action. If we need to fight or run, our body is putting us in the best physical condition it can for such a response. But what about when we are not in any physical danger? How does fear serve us when we are not being threatened?

For many, it can keep us from putting ourselves at risk of ridicule, embarrassment, or being singled out in a negative way. If we are fearful or uneasy in a situation, our ability to focus on what is going on around us can still come in handy, even if it isn't for defending our lives. Being more aware of the reactions and body language of those around us will give us a better indicator if someone is reacting poorly to an event. We can pick up the tone of what they are saying or catch on to the subtle hints in how they are conducting themselves. If they seem annoyed or anxious to leave, we can see that and act accordingly. This type of attention to detail can be extremely helpful in business or social situations. Being able to read a room and understand if events are moving in the right direction can help you avoid saying or doing the wrong thing. But it can also lead to the exact anxiety we are trying to avoid.

Often, when we suffer from anxiety, we become hypersensitive to people's reactions. We have a tendency to apply meaning to things where there may not be any. Suddenly, a woman shifting in a chair could cause us to assume she is getting bored with what we are saying, when in reality, she just needed to adjust herself for comfort.

Assigning meaning to things where there is none is a common trait for people with anxiety. We make assumptions, usually in a negative way, and read into things people do or say when there isn't anything to read into. This can cause an unnecessary level of fear and anxiety that does not serve us well. We need to be cautious about reading too much into events when we are feeling fear.

Asking that question – "How does this serve me?" – will help determine if it is actually serving you well or not at all. In that case, telling yourself that this fear does not serve me is an acceptable response. Letting yourself know you don't need to be afraid won't necessarily remove all fear, but it will at least allow yourself to know it is unnecessary and make your ability to relax a bit easier.

Question Three: What is the Best-Case Scenario?

Often, when people find themselves in stressful or fearful situations, they tend to envision the worst-case scenario. The mind of an anxious person is very creative when left to its own devices. It almost never moves in a positive direction in these situations. The best way to manage this negative thinking is to take back control and consciously redirect your thoughts into a more positive and beneficial direction.

Instead of thinking about what could go wrong, try asking yourself what could go right? What is the best-case scenario you could hope for? Keep your thoughts and mental focus on what can go right instead of what can go wrong, and you'll naturally begin to worry less and start to picture a more exciting future.

Visualization is an incredibly powerful tool. It can be used to create an amazing life, or it can be used to create a terrifying future. What made my dark room so terrifying was not what was hiding in the dark, but what I visualized hiding in the dark. The picture I created in my mind was far more frightening than the reality of my toys and dirty clothes on the floor. The reality was actually quite boring, but the image I held in my mind was far more terrifying. If I had closed my eyes and imagined puppies and kittens in my room, I bet I wouldn't have been half as afraid as I was.

Learning to see things working out in a positive way is key to creating a more positive outlook on life. When we picture everything going wrong, we often find that life lives up to our expectation. But I've personally found that when I learn to go into a situation visualizing it working out well, my life often rises to that level as well. So instead of expecting things to go wrong, spend your energy imagining them going right. You may just be surprised how often they do.

Question Four: Can I Face this Fear?

This is the most challenging question, but also the one that has the most upside. When you learn to face your fear, you'll begin to experience the reality of what it is like to confront your fears head on and see what it is like when you do. There is a sense of relief and empowerment when you begin to face what you fear and come out on the other side unscathed. Our fears are always so much more challenging in our own heads than they are in real life.

This doesn't mean that the fear we feel isn't real or challenging. It absolutely is. The fear we face can be a crippling reminder of all the bad things that have ever happened to us in our lives. Fear is one of the most powerful emotions we can experience. In fact, the majority of the decisions we make over the span of our entire life is made either from a place of love or a place of fear.

Learning to face our fears can be one of the most liberating experiences we'll ever know. It lifts the shackles we place on our lives and gives us a sense of power and freedom that many never realize.

And while this question can be scary and empowering, it can also be disheartening and defeating. When we can't face our fear, we are often very hard on ourselves. We beat up on ourselves, tell ourselves that we are not worthy, strong, or brave, and we treat ourselves with anger, hatred, and frustration. The truth is, when we can't face a fear, that is the time we need to be loving, kind, and supportive the most. Think of it as if you were talking to your best friend. If he came to you and said he didn't think he could do something, how would you respond?

Would you tell him that he is worthless and weak? Would you tell him that he needed to stop being such a baby and that he was a failure? Would you think poorly of him and not want to be around him anymore? If so, I don't think he is going to be your friend much longer.

You'd probably tell him that it would be okay. You might say that if he didn't think he could face that fear now, maybe he would be able to sometime in the future. If you did push him to face the fear, you would do it by encouraging him, telling him how strong and brave you know he can be. You might even tell him that you loved him and would always be there for him.

That is exactly what he would need to hear. And that is exactly what you also need to hear.

We need to learn how to be our own best own friends. We need to practice loving and supporting ourselves more. We need to be kind to ourselves, to treat ourselves with compassion and patience. And most of all, we need to support ourselves and have faith that we can overcome our fear because we are strong, even when we don't think we are.

Our inner dialogue is something we need to become more aware of, especially when we struggle with anxiety, fear, depression, or any other limiting belief or self-sabotaging behavior. The story we tell ourselves becomes the story of our life, both the past and the future. We need to learn how to love who we are and to support ourselves when we need it most. So if you can't face your fear right now, it's okay. Learning the art of positive self-talk will help get you there – when you are ready.

"Darkness cannot drive out darkness; only light can do that. Hate cannot drive out hate; only love can do that."
– Martin Luther King, Jr.

CHAPTER 11: HOW TO FORGIVE

This has been the most challenging chapter for me to write. It probably would have been written almost a full year earlier had it not been for my procrastination on this topic. I did not procrastinate because I felt forgiveness isn't a priority; it may be the most important thing we can do to live a happier life. It's because everything else I've written in this book has been based on issues I've faced and learned to overcome or resolve. Forgiveness is a topic I am still working on in my own life. And when I say "still working on," I mean it in the present tense.

As I write this, my father is lying in a hospital bed in Boston, Massachusetts. About two years ago, he started having pains in his stomach. He didn't have much of an appetite, and he was having trouble keeping food down. Of course, because he is stubborn and refuses to ask for help, he kept this hidden from us. Eventually, it got so bad that his ego was forced to take a back seat, and he went to the doctor. After a few days and many tests, they discovered his liver was beginning to fail. They couldn't be sure exactly what happened or why. He hadn't been a big drinker from what I remembered of him – a beer or two after work, but never more than that. But in truth, I hadn't spent much time with him over the past few years and couldn't honestly speak to how he spent his days after retirement.

Leaving the police force was hard for him. It wasn't his choice. He would have stayed an officer until his last day if he could. He loved his job, and it gave him purpose. In many ways, it was his first love – maybe his only true love. Through five children, two divorces, and multiple on-the-side businesses, being a police officer was the one constant in his life. But after a hip surgery, two bad knees, and a bad shoulder, this chapter of his life would come to an end at the ripe young age of 65.

In many ways, I always felt his family took a backseat to his job. Not because he didn't love his family, but because I believe he felt that he was at his best when he was on the job. Most nights at dinnertime, he was in his full uniform and the police cruiser was running in the driveway while we ate. Eventually his radio would crackle, he'd respond, head out the door, and that would be it.

He worked 3 to 11 p.m. most nights while running a construction company during the day. He plowed driveways during the winter and worked traffic details on his days off. He was gone in the morning before we got up and didn't come home until after we were asleep. In short, we didn't see much of him growing up, and part of me resented him for it. He did his best to make time when he could, and we went on vacation every summer. He would take us out to play mini-golf and eat ice cream. He taught me how to fish. When he was there, he was there. But often he wasn't.

As I got older, my resentment grew. He got remarried and had two more children. In many ways, I felt like I had been replaced. Rumors swirled of other women – nothing stays quiet when you live in a small town. Some people had some not-so-nice things to say about him, and my mother – his first wife – was often vocal with her opinions. She always blamed him for their divorce. She claimed he was a cheater and a liar. A common insult around the house was that "you're just like your father."

When I was little, I idolized my father. I thought he was a superhero, and I wanted to be just like him. But by the time I was in my thirties, I was working hard to be nothing like him while trying to resolve the love I still held for him in my heart. He had ruined his second marriage, fathered a child with another woman, and was almost broke. When he was forced into retirement, he could no longer hide from his mistakes and broken relationships – they were all he had left.

So did that make him drink? Maybe. I don't know. He's never told me, and I've never asked.

All I do know is that in 2015 he ended up in the hospital. When the doctors diagnosed him with cirrhosis of the liver, we were all shocked. And while I was concerned for his health, I was also angry with him. Angry for how things turned out with him and my mom, for not making more time for his family, for cheating on his wives, for making me feel like I wasn't good enough for him, and even angry that, after all the things he had done, I still loved him and didn't want to lose him.

That anger kept me away. I would call every few months and check in on him, but mostly I would connect with my brothers and sister to see what they knew. As much as I wanted to be with him, I didn't want to see him. My anger was keeping me from fixing my relationship with him, and I didn't know what to do. Instead of talking to him, I avoided talking to him. The avoidance turned into guilt, and that guilt fed the fire of my anger. I blamed him for making me want to stay away. For being sick. For the pain I felt – both then and now.

Two months ago. I was sitting at my desk at work and my phone buzzed. I looked at the caller ID and saw it was my dad.

My stomach flipped, and I didn't answer it. He left me a message asking me to give him a call. I texted him to say I'd call him in the morning.

After dinner that night, I got a text from my older brother, Pat.

"Did u speak with Dad today?"

"Texted him to say I'd call him in the morning. What's up? Everything ok?"

"No. MRI results came in."

"Call me."

I got Pat on the phone, and he informed me that the latest liver tests came back.

"Dad has liver cancer. He had found out the week before and was calling us all to let us know."

My dad called me to tell me he had cancer, and I didn't pick up the phone. What kind of horrible person does that? Why was I still so angry with him?

I hung up the phone in shock. It was too late to call my dad, so I decided I would wait and call him in the morning. I didn't want to make the call. I didn't want to hear him tell me he had cancer. I knew it was a point of no return. Once he said it, it would be true. There would be no turning back.

I called him. We talked. I did my best to not let on that I knew. He told me that he would fight and that he didn't want me to worry or let the news ruin my day. I didn't want to cry. I didn't want him to worry about me because I was worried about him.

We talked a couple minutes more, but I can't really remember what we said. I told him I loved him, and we hung up. And sitting alone in my office at work, I broke down and cried.

We've spent the past few months doing tests and getting ready for procedures. Terms like "quality of life" and "comfortable" have been passed around. Was this really happening?

Suddenly, I'm a little kid again. Back in that familiar place, filled with anxiety, worried that my dad is going to die and I am powerless to do anything about it. The difference now is that I'm no longer anxious about what might happen, but anxious about what is happening. There is no longer any "what if" in this scenario, only when. His liver is failing. He has cancer. He is dying. It may take a few weeks, a few months, or even a few years. I just don't know.

I'm not going to lie to you: Death has the ability to speed up the forgiveness process. There is something about having to face this reality that forces our hand and compels us to take action in a way we might otherwise be hesitant to take. I know this is true for me with regard to my father. He is going to die, not someday in the future but someday soon. If I don't resolve this now, I will never resolve it.

This idea that we have time, that we can eventually work things out, is part of what keeps us stuck in so many aspects of our life. We feel as if we have time. Time to say we are sorry, to tell someone how we feel, to reach out and connect with someone we've lost touch with, or time to make things right. And in many ways, we do have time.

That is, until that time runs out.

Time is a source of measurement. It measures distance, but rather than measuring the physical distance between two points in space, time measures the distance between two moments. We use seconds, minutes, days, and years much in the same way we use inches, feet, and miles. Moments are not fixed in space like physical objects. We know there are 2,789 miles between Boston, Massachusetts, and Los Angeles, California. Knowing distance allows us to accurately plan our travel between two places. We know how far we need to drive, how much gas we would need for our car, how many meals we would need to eat on our journey, even the amount of time it would take to get from one place to another.

But unlike other measurements of distance between two fixed places, the time between two moments is not fixed. And that means we cannot accurately measure the distance between them. Sure, we can plan on being someplace at 8 a.m. or 2 p.m. and use a clock to make sure we are "on time" and not "late." We can even project how many days, months, or years we have between the moment we are currently in and those we'd like to experience in the future – getting married, having children, or retiring from our job. But we have no idea if that amount of time needed to reach our future moment will be available to us when we need it. We have no way of knowing how much time we have left in our lives because we don't know the amount of time that exists between the start and end of our experience here on earth – the time between our birth and death. This makes planning our journey a lot more challenging.

When it comes to many aspects in our lives, including forgiving others, we always feel as though we have time to do it… someday. Why do today what you can put off until tomorrow, right? The problem is when our time is up, it often happens with little warning and no chance of going back. The destination is final. If there was something you wanted to get done before your ride was over – too bad! You had your chance, but your time has run out. It's almost like driving a car with no gas gauge to tell you how much fuel you have left. You get in the car and start driving. Most of us try not to think about what will happen when we run out of gas. We drive all over town, never worried that someday our tank will be empty. Some drive fast, enjoying the trip, because they know it could end at any moment. Others avoid leaving their driveways or the safety of their neighborhood out of fear that driving too far could end their trip prematurely. But make no mistake: No matter how you treat your car or how far you travel, your tank will eventually run out and your joyride through life will be over.

For this reason, when something happens that tips you off that the end of the journey is near – either for yourself or for someone else – the pressure to resolve situations often supersedes your tendency to procrastinate. The number of tomorrows becomes limited, forcing you to take action today. And there is nothing like an approaching deadline to force you to stop procrastinating and start taking necessary action.

But when we are talking about forgiving others, knowing you need to take action doesn't help if you don't know what action you need to take. What is forgiveness, anyway? And why is it often so hard to forgive people for what they've done?

First, let me be clear about something. Talking about having limited time and the desire to forgive before it is too late is not intended to pressure you into thinking you need to forgive everyone for anything they've ever done. Yes, time can become a factor when forgiving someone, but going through the process of forgiving someone takes time – sometimes more than you have left. You must allow yourself to go through the range of emotions surrounding what happened before you can reach a point where you are ready to forgive. Rushing to forgive someone too quickly can actually lead to feeling more resentment and anger rather than less.

When we forgive someone before we are ready, we do a disservice to our own emotional health. This is not to say that forgiving someone has to be a long or drawn-out process. But if we do not go through the healing process fully and completely, we won't actually let go of the anger we feel inside. And that is actually what it means to forgive – to let go of the anger and pain you hold inside yourself. Forgiveness is an inside job.

Forgiving people does not mean what they did was acceptable. It does not justify their actions or their intent. Forgiveness isn't about the other person's actions. Forgiveness is about healing yourself of the burden of carrying around the negative emotions caused by the action.

Most of us tell someone that they are forgiven before we've actually put down the emotional attachment to what has happened. No matter what someone has done, if it generates pain, sadness, anger, or doubt within our being, it must be processed and dealt with completely before we can find ourselves in a position to actually forgive.

Most people forgive for all the wrong reasons. Many feel that they are supposed to forgive because it's the right thing to do. Haven't we always been told to forgive and forget? To let bygones be bygones? We don't want to be seen as someone who holds a grudge. We want to be seen as a loving and forgiving person in the eyes of society, so we try to forgive others, even when we don't truly feel like forgiving them. There is pressure on us at times to be the "bigger person" and to forgive those who have wronged us. After all, the more forgiving we are, the better person we are, right?

Sometimes the act of forgiving others is done out of a desire to be viewed as a good person by others rather than as a healing act for ourselves. We try to control the opinions of others through our actions, attempting to dictate how the world sees us. We do what we think the world wants us to do rather than what we feel in our hearts, because we think if others like us, we will like ourselves. It is a process of fixing yourself by changing how the outside world perceives you. But this never works because we cannot control the outside world. We can only control ourselves, and even that is a challenge at times.

For others, the idea of forgiving someone seems almost insulting unless the person who is in the wrong does some form of penance in order to prove they deserve forgiveness. Without such a sufficient act, we tend to hold on to our anger and resentment toward this person while feeling completely justified in our righteous indignation. We deserve to be made whole, and, until that day comes, forgiveness will be withheld indefinitely.

But no matter which person you are – the type that forgives everyone or that forgives no one – you may find that neither action seems to make you feel better about what happened. You may find that you keep replaying what was said or done, over and over in your mind, reliving the pain, the heartache, the trauma, and the hurt for a much longer time than the actual event even took place. It is amazing how a passing word or action can often leave a lasting mark – sometimes a permanent one.

Learning to forgive is difficult because most of us look at

forgiveness in the wrong way. We make it about the other people. We give our power away, hoping they will do or say the words that will allow us to forgive them. If we want to truly learn to forgive, we must learn to honor and be true to ourselves first.

This is the secret behind forgiveness that most people miss. The truth that makes letting go of all the pain, hurt, and resentment caused by others so difficult. This is the one aspect that most people miss when trying to forgive someone for what they've done or said.

In order to fully forgive someone else, you must first learn to forgive yourself.

Now, this does not mean that what happened was your fault or that in some way you deserved what happened. Often the words and actions of others can shape and mold our own perception of who we think we are, especially when these things happen when we are very young.

As children, we are born into a world where we have no idea if what is around us is positive or negative. We are all born with a clean slate. But from the very first interaction we have with our new world, we begin to process and apply meaning to things. We begin to learn, understand, experience, and process. We know that we feel things – hunger, temperature, pain, and discomfort – yet we don't realize we are the ones feeling them. We have no sense of self early on. When a baby looks into a mirror, they have no idea that it is their own reflection they are looking at. It isn't until around 18 months that a baby begins to understand the idea of self. The idea that the reflection they see in the mirror is not another baby but their own reflection. For the first time, they are aware that they exist. Before that moment, everything experienced was describing elements of our outer world. But now we begin the process of building our inner world. Personalities become more pronounced, choices become more deliberate, and we begin to build our sense of who we are as individuals.

Those lucky enough to come from loving, supportive families develop a sense of self that is rich with positive qualities. Children learn to be confident, feel loved and cared for, and are safe and secure in their lives. Others who do not get the same level of love and affection may begin to see themselves as less confident, longing for the feeling of love and support and desiring a sense of safety that may otherwise be missing. As both types of children grow, this sense of self becomes more and more ingrained in their perception of the person they are and how they fit into the world around them. This becomes the basis for how they see themselves and shapes the choices they make as teenagers, young adults, and adults.

For me, my childhood left me feeling insecure and scared. I know my parents loved me, but their love seemed to have strings attached. My brother and I seemed to always be in the middle of their fighting and forced to take sides. Love wasn't something you gave freely; it was something you had to earn. And in my family, you earned it by picking one parent over the other. This created a sense of instability in me that they could never have predicted. I doubted my abilities and felt like I was never enough: never good enough, smart enough, or talented enough. This self-doubt led to a host of issues that caused my life to spiral out of control. And for many years, I blamed my parents for everything that was wrong in my life. I was angry with them for being so selfish and self-centered in how they raised me. Why didn't they love me enough to put me first? Why didn't they care that every time we moved from house to house or town to town, I was the one who was suffering? Why wasn't my happiness important to them? What did I do to deserve this life?

I'd like to tell you that once I began addressing my anxiety and rebuilding my life that these feelings went away. That when I learned to love myself and value my abilities, the feelings of anger and betrayal faded into a soft love of understanding and peace. I'd like to tell you that, but I can't. Like I said in the beginning of this chapter, forgiveness is challenging and something I continue to work on.

What I can tell you is that as my understanding of myself has grown, so has my understanding of my parents. My compassion for what I went through and how it shaped my life slowly began to seep into my relationships with my parents. It became easier for me to see them, not simply as two parents whose choices had a negative impact on me, but as two people who struggled to make choices for themselves. Much of what they did had more to do with how they felt about themselves than it did about how they felt about me. I wasn't the cause of their problems, I was just part of the fallout that resulted from their lives.

They loved me the best way they could, the only way they could. It was all they knew how to do. It didn't make their actions right, nor did it excuse some of the choices they made, but it did open up my ability to let go of the guilt, anger, and resentment I've felt toward them. I've learned to forgive them by learning to forgive myself. I am not to blame for their lives, nor are they fully to blame for mine. Sure, they may not have set me up for easy success. I may not have had all the advantages or the blinding self-confidence I see in people I admire. Some parents build their kids up to the point of starting life from the top of the mountain positive. I felt a bit more like my parents dug a big negative hole and dropped me into it. But I've learned a couple things from being at the bottom of that hole.

I've learned that when you are stuck in a hole, you cannot get out by continuing to dig the hole someone else started. More negativity just makes the hole deeper. You need to stop digging. This means that you need to do the work to rebuild who you are in your own eyes. This entire book is based on the idea that how we see ourselves shapes our reality. If you've been doing the work up until this point, you've hopefully begun to experience some of the benefits associated with changing how you define yourself and how you speak to yourself. Rebuilding your self-confidence and self-esteem is like putting dirt back into the hole. You begin to fill it back in, and then you can begin to climb out.

Another thing I learned from getting out of that hole is that I know no matter what holes I fall into in the future, I have the ability to get myself out. I've done it before, and I can do it again. And knowing you have that skill is a life-changer.

That's why I'm writing this book. I feel it's part of my life's purpose to help others learn to get out of their own holes rather than just be angry at the people who started digging them.

And to do this, we must be willing to look deep inside and be honest with how we feel within our heart – how the other person made us feel. Often what we feel in these situations is sadness, pain, or hurt, which leads to feeling a deep sense of rejection or worthlessness. These emotions are difficult for us to process because we don't have a lot of experience with them. Not to say we don't feel these emotions enough. It's that when we do feel them, we do whatever we can to avoid them. Most people do everything they can to suppress these feelings when they arise, often choosing instead to convert them into an emotion they are more comfortable in processing.

None of what I've accomplished over the years would have been possible if I wasn't willing to look deep within myself and face the things I had hidden away for so long. Like that 18-month-old baby looking into a mirror, I had to stop looking at someone else and start looking at myself. When I stopped feeling the pain, guilt, and fear of what went on in my life, I stopped holding my parents responsible for causing it. By forgiving myself, I learned to forgive them.

But looking deep inside with a willingness to face the emotions is only one part of the process. The other part is recognizing that emotions are very rarely singular in nature. They are complex and overlapping and can even masquerade as other emotions that you find easier to deal with. We must learn to unmask our emotions before we can fully deal with them. This is the true challenge with forgiveness.

For me, whenever I would feel hurt or upset, my subconscious would convert those feelings into anger. It was easier for me to be angry at what someone else did rather than dealing with how

I felt as a result of their actions. This redirection of emotions is a type of self-preservation. No one likes to be hurt – physically or emotionally. By feeling anger toward my parents, it protected me from feeling the pain of rejection that was at the heart of my emotions. I could focus on them instead of on me. This kept me protected in the short term, but it did far more damage in the long term. This process of redirecting emotions becomes a habit that we are often completely unaware of. Much like what we've talked about in previous chapters, if you repeat an action or behavior enough, the response eventually happens on a subconscious level. In order to really process your emotions, you have to unpack the emotion you are feeling.

American professor and psychologist Robert Plutchik presented a theory of emotion that stated there were only eight primary emotions a person could experience: joy, sadness, trust, disgust, fear, anger, surprise, and anticipation. He believed that our complete emotional spectrum could be made up from different levels and combinations of these eight emotions. As an example, rage would be a stronger version of anger while annoyance would be a lesser version. An emotion like disapproval is actually a combination of both surprise and sadness.

All of these emotions are designed to help us survive and stay safe, at our most basic level as human beings. If you see something that causes you to feel fear, there is a good chance it is something that might do you harm and you would naturally want to avoid it. The emotion is designed to elicit a physical response: I feel fear so I avoid the situation. So when we feel an emotion, we often react without thinking. This is because it is the designed function of that emotion to get us to take action.

But why is it so important to understand that emotion, and why does that impact our ability to forgive? The answer lies in our ability to work backward and deconstruct the scenario, to reframe it in a way that will allow us to better let go of the emotional attachment to the situation that started the process. Because often, the story we tell ourselves feeds into the emotions we are feeling and causes us to build up the story even more in our minds. If we can learn to reframe that story and bring it into a different light, we can begin to shift the emotional response and alleviate its hold on us.

One of my favorite Buddhist teachings is the story of a monk who was returning home along a narrow path late one evening. As he walked, he noticed something on the path. He leaned in to inspect it. He noticed the item was long, thin, and coiled. He withdrew in fright, realizing it was a snake. "How am I going to get home with my path blocked by this snake?" he thought to himself. "What if it is poisonous?" His fear quickly turned to terror at the prospect of being bitten by such a deadly creature. The monk remembered that he had some fire-making elements on him from his travel and quickly fashioned himself a torch to light his path. He placed the flame close to the snake only to discover there was no snake but a small section of rope in the path. His fear quickly turned to amusement when he realized there was never any danger on his path other than the illusion he had created in his mind.

This story of the monk and the rope illustrates many aspects of anxiety, fear, and how we often create our own illusions of danger on our path. The monk could have chosen to run the other way or even sit in fear and do nothing, hoping the snake would act first and clear the way for him to pass. This is very similar to what we do in our lives. We see a snake instead of a rope, and then we avoid it or simply wait to see if the snake will get out of our way.

For me, the pain generated from my childhood was real. But the story surrounding it was built up in my mind. I turned the rope into a snake by creating reasons why it happened. I wanted to blame someone for what happened. My mother blamed my father, my father blamed my mother, and I blamed them both. But I also blamed myself, not directly, but indirectly. I always felt like I might be able to make them happy if I could do or say the right thing at the right time. If I agreed with my mother and blamed my father, she would be happy. Or if I agreed with my father and blamed my mother, he would be happy. Their fighting wasn't a result of my actions, but since I couldn't make them happy, I must be to blame in some way. I internalized what happened and allowed it to define me as a person.

Even after I began deconstructing the story of my childhood in my mind, I still wanted to blame someone. If I would no longer blame myself, I would have to blame them. I wanted my parents to apologize to me for what happened, but in looking back, in many ways, they already had. But their apologies didn't make my hurt go away, so I couldn't forgive them. How could I still be mad at them if they were really sorry for what had happened? I assumed they must not have really meant it since it didn't fix how I felt inside. But they did mean it. I know they did.

The truth was, I was hurting because there was still pain there. I had over thirty years of pain, anger, and blame that had built up inside me. That doesn't just magically go away because someone says "sorry." It takes time to heal and rebuild a relationship – with others and yourself.

Time: It's the one thing my dad and I are now running out of.

So what does this all mean? How do we go about learning to forgive others, and, more importantly, how do we go about learning to forgive ourselves?

The first part requires us to focus on being mindfully aware of how we feel and why we feel this way. By mindfully observing our emotions, we can apply a more rational reasoning behind the rise of the emotion, thus allowing us to better control how we want to react rather than responding out of instinct.

These emotions impact our ability to forgive if we are not completely clear as to why we feel the way we do. Our emotions are often a combination of multiple emotions. We need to sit and understand which emotions are at play before we can fully understand how to process them, experience them, and eventually let them go. We need to learn how to unpack our emotions to know which ones we are dealing with. This ability – to be honest about what we are feeling – will predict how well we can heal and forgive.

Once we've opened up to our emotions and learned to process how we feel, we can begin to open up space for understanding and compassion for those we feel contributed to our hurt. Those we feel we should forgive need to be included in our process of healing and letting go.

Forgiveness does not mean you approve of what the other person did. As we all know, some people have been subjected to cruel acts of abuse, brutality, and even torture. Learning to forgive someone who has committed acts like rape, assault, and murder is something completely different, although much of what is here can still be applied. In such extreme cases, seeking help from a professional therapist to deal with the trauma associated with such events is always recommended.

I am also not suggesting what I went through even comes close to some of the tragedies you may have experienced. All I am suggesting is that, whatever the type or severity of pain you carry, it only serves to hurt you the longer you carry it. The Buddhist philosophy teaches, "You will not be punished for your anger, you will be punished by your anger."

You may have every right to be angry for what someone did. You may be completely justified in feeling hate, anger, and resentment toward another person. They may have done something so unspeakable that they could spend the rest of their life trying to make amends and always fall short. But in the end, the anger you carry will be yours and yours alone. It will burden you, limit you, and negatively impact you and all your relationships moving forward. But if you can learn to let go of that anger, process the emotions associated with what took place, and move past those feelings, you will liberate yourself from your suffering and experience a freedom you've been keeping from yourself for far too long. And the only way to let go of what you feel is to allow yourself to feel it.

Forgiving someone isn't about making someone apologize for what they did – although that helps – it's about learning to love who you are enough to give yourself the gift of freedom from carrying the pain that's holding you back. It's a way of moving forward without carrying that weight. And as you move forward, it is perfectly acceptable to establish new rules and boundaries for those who have hurt you. Keeping people in your life that you must repeatedly forgive is a recipe for lifelong suffering. When you learn to value yourself, you will quickly learn that constantly exposing yourself to negativity is not a healthy way to exist. Do not send others away in anger or with bad intent. Simply work to make peace with the situation and focus on moving forward – with or without them.

As my father's time continues to run short, I am grateful to share these last moments with him. We've talked more in the past few months than we have in years. He is my father, my hero. He may not have been the perfect father, the perfect husband, or the perfect man, but he'll always be my dad. The man who taught me to fish, ride a bike, fight fair, be respectful, work hard, and never back down from a challenge is now teaching me how to forgive, how to fight through the pain, how to keep smiling, and how to say goodbye to someone you love.

"It is during out darkest moments that we must focus to see the light."
– Aristotle

CHAPTER 12: FOCUSING YOUR MIND

"Watch this," he said to me as he held the glass still.

One of the kids from the neighborhood was sitting in the dirt on the sidewalk.

"What are you doing?" I asked with the curiosity of a three-year-old – fitting, since that was about my age.

"Just watch."

In his hand, he held a large, black-framed magnifying glass. Between his legs, he had constructed a pile of dried leaves and twigs. He moved the magnifying glass up and down, above the makeshift pile of kindling. I could see a round, bright spotlight that appeared on the pile, which changed shape as he moved it closer and farther away. He moved the magnifying glass into a position that caused the circle to become quite small and intensely bright in the center of a large leaf in the pile.

I sat and watched, not exactly sure what I was supposed to be waiting for. Suddenly, a small line of smoke began to rise up from the very spot in which the light was touching the leaf. A moment later, the leaf burst into flames right before my eyes, right there on the sidewalk.

"Wow," I said in amazement. "How'd you do that?"

He grinned and responded, "Magic."

Of course, at the time, I believed it really was magic. I didn't understand the science behind how the magnifying glass bent the sunlight, causing it to become focused onto a concentrated spot on the leaf resulting in the temperature rising to a point high enough to cause the leaf to catch fire.

Our minds are very much like that magnifying glass. We know there is sunlight around us all day long, but we don't all spontaneously combust when we walk outside into the sunlight. (Not unless you're a vampire, of course.)

The sunlight that lights up our days and warms our planet does so because it is dispersed over the entire world. If the light became focused into one sharp beam, it would most likely act like a laser and do massive damage to both our planet and to us. The fact that the light exists isn't the dangerous part, but how focused that light becomes can be. How we focus our thoughts can be just as warming – and as dangerous.

One of the greatest challenges for people who suffer from stress, anxiety, and fear is learning how to focus their mind, thoughts, and attention on what they choose to focus on, rather than simply on what is available for them to focus on. There is no shortage of things available for our minds to become distracted by or fixated on. Everything around us is a possible draw for our focus. Our lives have become one giant distraction, causing many to feel as if the world is pulling them in a specific direction rather than having the free will to choose their own path.

From the phones in our pockets, to the shows on television, to the constant bombardment of advertisements around us, our everyday experience has become one of constant assault on our senses to the point of dulling everything down to a subtle hum. Our ability to simply sit and relax has become a challenge and a battle of wills over our need for technological interaction with the rest of the world.

We consume at an alarming rate. This consumption isn't limited to what we eat or items we purchase to make ourselves feel better. It also includes the large amount of digital and audio consumption. These things have become available to us with such ease and frequency that it is almost impossible for some people to get out of bed in the morning before they've read a tweet, updated a status, liked an image, or been influenced by a meme.

Our smartphones have become our alarm clocks. For many, including myself, it is far too easy to turn off the alarm and then turn on the noise of social media. I would start my day staring into a small, electronic glowing screen, consuming opinions, emotions, ideas, and advertisements, all designed to make me think less and consume more.

And while it may seem that this change in technology has happened suddenly and without warning, it's actually been going on for a long time. The internet went live on August 6, 1991, laying the foundation for our current communication explosion. Personal computers had been around since the early '80s but their daily use was limited until the technology became more affordable and available to average consumers. But don't be fooled into thinking smartphones and social media caused our focus issues. Before every home had a computer and the internet, we had televisions to keep us distracted.

According to Mitchell Stephens, a professor at New York University, there were approximately 6,000 television sets in American homes in 1946, but by 1951, that number exploded to 12 million. By 1955, half the homes in the country had a television set.[1] Before television, families would listen to the radio for

---

[1] "History of Television," New York University, accessed January 20, 2018, https://www.nyu.edu/classes/stephens/History%20of%20Television%20page.htm.

entertainment and news. And prior to that, books and newspapers kept people informed.

So while this isn't the first time our focus has been challenged by changes in technology, it's hard to argue that transitioning from having radios and televisions in our homes to having them in our pockets has greatly increased our ability for distraction. The need for improved mental focus has never been more challenged and more needed than in today's society.

Now don't get me wrong. I am part of this same world that many of you are. This isn't a call to abandon all technology and live like monks on the top of a mountain. Far from it. I believe we have a responsibility to ourselves to learn to live in our world rather than hide away from it. Technology is a tool. And just like any other tool, it can be used to improve the quality of our lives when used properly and it can be a source of great destruction when used irresponsibly.

But how can we be expected to master the technological tools of today if we've never learned how to use the most advanced piece of technology that exists right inside each one of us?

That technology is our minds.

We are only now beginning to scratch the surface of what our brains are capable of. For years, we believed our brains were hardwired to function a certain way. Each one of us seemed born with a pre-installed program that we lived at the mercy of. But science has now taught us this way of looking at the brain is not accurate. Our minds can change and grow based on how we use them. They are not hardwired, but rather plastic and flexible. This neuroplasticity means we can actually reprogram our brains to function in new and more beneficial ways, and that our minds are not limited by genetics, but they're rather limitless. Our minds are shaped by how we use them. And if they can be taught to function in a certain way due to what they are exposed to, that also means we can change how they function by controlling their exposure. We have the ability to reshape how our brain works and thinks if we are willing to take responsibility for how it currently functions and, more importantly, learn to control what our mind is exposed to moving forward. By understanding how our brain works, we can learn to control it, but first we must become aware and accept our role in how our brain works today.

Now, I am not a neurologist. I am not going to even attempt to explain the brain to you in this book. My goal for this book is to introduce you to the idea that we have more control over our mind than we realize and we must take responsibility for how we use it.

The mind needs to be trained like any other part of our body. Learning to focus and avoid distractions is a skill just like anything else you've ever learned. Learning how to walk, talk, eat, or throw a ball took time and practice for us to excel at. Learning to control the focus of our thoughts takes just as much time, practice, and discipline as any other skill we want to learn.

When we look at someone who goes to the gym and works out, it is easy to see the changes that take place. A thinner waist, bigger biceps, stronger shoulders, and a toned, healthy-looking physique can be seen with the eyes. The muscles are hard to the touch and their body is tighter and less soft than the body of someone who does not work out.

When we are not in good shape, we can both see and feel it as well. From the way our clothes fit to seeing ourselves in the mirror and thinking, "I need to get into better shape," there is no shortage of visual and/or physical indications when we need to put down the doughnuts and go for a walk. We can look at and touch our body at any time to see how in shape or out of shape it has gotten. The ease of access to such information makes it much more apparent when we need to do more than get our physical health in order. But what about our mental health?

We don't ever see our brain. We can't look at it in the mirror and notice when it isn't being exercised enough. If our gray matter is beginning to atrophy and shrink, we have no way of knowing this is taking place. If parts of our mind are too active and other parts are not active enough, we can't use our sense of touch or sight to see these issues. We never stand in front of a mirror after getting out of the shower or while trying on bathing suits and say how out of shape our brain looks!

The only way we can tell if our brains are healthy and working properly is to "look" at how we are feeling, thinking, processing information, and dealing with our emotional states. This requires us to be more self-aware of how we think, feel, act, and process information. But there is a challenge here that most never consider. How is it that we can become intellectually aware of how we think if the process of thinking is handled and influenced by the involuntary machinery that makes up the engine of our thoughts? How can we outthink the very brain that is responsible for them?

As mentioned in previous chapters, becoming the watcher of our thoughts becomes a key component in the process of outthinking our brains. If we are to get a better handle on how our thoughts impact our life, we need to break free from the idea that we, in some way, are our thoughts. Instead, we need to cultivate the practice of being aware of the involuntary thinking as it takes place, recognize the patterns that this type of thinking creates, and interrupt the pattern so we may redirect our thoughts in a new and more beneficial direction.

I think one of the biggest misconceptions of meditation is the idea that your mind goes quiet. I don't believe this is ever the case. What I've experienced is not that my mind ever goes quiet, giving up the action of thinking. Rather, my mind becomes focused on the quiet space between the thoughts. As it focuses on the quiet, it takes on the qualities of itself being quiet. But in truth, the mind is still very much thinking. It just happens to be thinking about being quiet.

The focus of the mind has been taken off the tasks of the day, the fears of tomorrow, and the regrets of yesterday. It isn't lost in the things I need to buy at the store, the bills I have to pay that month, or the projects that are due at work before 5 p.m.

During my meditation, my mind becomes focused on none of those things. It essentially becomes focused on nothing, or *no thing*. It turns its ever-watchful gaze on the silence of the moment, the empty canvas before the creator, the still air before the breeze. There is an understanding that this space of quiet emptiness is only a temporary existence. Its reprieve from the world is only fleeting. But as long as my mind is focused on this moment of peace, it continues to be my entire universe.

That is the power of learning: to focus your mind rather than let it run free with no control and no restrictions. It will go wherever it chooses, and you will feel as if you are being pulled along for the ride.

And when your mind's default setting for thought is one of negativity or fear, that is the direction it will most willingly travel.

It's true that some people have a much more positive outlook. So for them, the random movement of the mind tends to pull them in directions that are light, joyful, and pleasant. For others who are more creatively expressive with their thoughts, the mind spends time expressing itself through creative problem solving, whether it is with numbers, paints, or complex theories.

But for those of us whose attention is on survival, on not wanting to be singled out in a negative way, or searching for safety, comfort, and security in a world that seems to offer few of these things, our mind's default setting is one of finding the problems before they find us. For every solution, there is another problem. For every positive outcome, there is a negative one waiting for us to let our guard down.

This type of thinking isn't always a bad thing. There is nothing inherently good or bad when it comes to the tools we use, only in the way in which we use them. Our negative, fearful thinking is necessary when we find ourselves in a true, life-or-death situation. The problem is, the number of situations that are truly life or death are almost non-existent compared to the number of times our mind convinces us we are in danger. The mind is trained to look for the problem so it can be ready to react and respond when necessary. This constant vigilance is exhausting and causes us to never be able to relax and enjoy life. Our lives become a constant environment of stress, worry, and fear. We feel completely on edge and afraid all the time, and we are no longer even consciously aware of what it is we are afraid of. Everything is seen as a threat, so we always feel threatened.

For so many years, I would wake up and the first thing I would experience is a twisted, uneasy feeling in my stomach. I wouldn't have even opened my eyes fully or sat up in my bed. My mind had already decided there was something I needed to worry about, so it had started the process of making me anxious.

I used to get this feeling a lot in school before a big test. The problem is, when you suffer with anxiety, there is no relief from the feeling. In school, eventually you would take the test, and no matter if you passed or failed, the test would be done. With anxiety, there was never a test to be taken, so the feeling never went away. The test was every next second of every next day, so there was always something ahead of you to fear.

What we don't realize is that our brains function this way because we've trained them to focus on things in this manner. We've trained our minds to look for the fearful moments that threaten our peace, never understanding that it is the constant search for the threat we must focus on that is what is actually robbing us from our peaceful moments. It isn't the existence of the outside threat that causes us to fear, but our constant focus on the outside threat that is the fear itself. Fear is created inside of ourselves through the act of magnifying our focus.

The practice of meditation, which I hope you've been practicing since reading Chapter 4, will help you strengthen your ability to calm and focus your mind when it is necessary. This is not always easy to do, especially if you suffer from a severe disorder that impacts the overactivity or underactivity of certain parts of the brain, or if you have experienced a traumatic brain injury requiring medical attention or medication.

As I've stated before, I am not a doctor or licensed psychologist. I do not advise on matters regarding medications, their effectiveness, or their necessity given a specific disorder. My take on it has always been the same. Each person is an individual with a unique brain, which may or may not respond to treatments the same way others do. I do not suggest the use or non-use of any medications, but instead I simply make this suggestion: If you'd like to learn more about possible medical treatments, you should consult your physician, psychologist, psychiatrist, or counselor who is more familiar with your specific situation, medical history, and best course of treatment.

But even if you are or are not using medication, the tools and practices in this book will help you develop the strategies to lay a new groundwork to manage your thinking and approach your life in a new way. Learning to better control your thinking and becoming more mindful can be life-changing. I know it was for me.

The more you practice meditation and mindfulness, the easier you will find it to notice your thought patterns and recognize how they are impacting your current situation. Once you develop that skill, the next part is to begin to understand how to reframe your thoughts so you can redirect where your thoughts are taking you emotionally.

One of the greatest challenges most people face when dealing with anxiety, depression, or any barriers that keep them from creating their most authentic life is exactly how their thoughts impact all of those outcomes. If we were simply a rational, thought-driven species, we would have no problems doing what we wanted to do, creating what we wanted to create, and living lives that suited us best. We would be cold and calculating, making choices that were best for us in the moment and never looking back. But we have another part of our mentality that is closely connected to our thinking that makes us different from almost all other living things on this planet. Our thoughts generate something inside of us that have the ability to override our rational minds and hijack our lives in ways we are often unaware of. These are our emotions.

Emotions are funny things. They are neither right nor wrong. They are simply experienced. We cannot control our emotions any more than we can control other functions in our body. We don't consciously make our hearts beat or our stomachs process and break down food. These actions are referred to in biology as autonomic, or involuntary actions. When something happens that causes an emotional response, we are often taken for an emotional ride that we have no way of controlling. These emotions can heighten the importance of a given moment, causing our minds to better store the memory of that moment due to the significance our emotions place on it.

Almost every long-term memory that has been created in your mind is a combination of the facts of the moment combined with an elevated emotional state. This is why we don't tend to remember every single day in our lives but certain days stand out. Days that are of special meaning to us – such as our wedding day, the birth of a child, the passing of a loved one, or a national tragedy – tend to stay etched in our minds in great detail because our emotional state in that moment added significance that causes it to stand out against the other less significant days we experience.

Anxiety and fear are emotions just like love and excitement. They are generated when our experience and our thoughts combine in a way that triggers an emotional response within our body. The excitement of falling in love can feel just as uncomfortable to someone as a panic attack. Our hearts race, we start to feel hot, we sweat and get that butterfly feeling in the pit of our stomach. This reaction is a common response for both fear and excitement. Our ability to recognize this feeling as something we enjoy or something we want to avoid often depends on the thoughts we think and the expectations we apply to the possible outcome of that situation. The combination of thought and emotion drives our lives and dictates the decisions we make in almost every moment. But often we are not consciously aware of the connection of these elements, so we feel as if life is happening to us rather than seeing the active role we play.

If we can become more consciously, mindfully aware of this connection between thought and emotion, and learn to recognize what triggers create emotional responses, we can learn to apply a more rational understanding to what feels like a very irrational response. Developing the skills to control our thoughts will empower us with the ability to shift our thinking from thoughts that generate negative emotions to thoughts that generate more positive ones. Learning to shift your thinking will alter your emotional state, thus allowing you to harness the powerful combination of thought and emotion and use it for your creative advantage.

But if it's so easy, why don't more people do this? It's because we are never taught how to use our minds or to understand our emotions. For many people, emotions are repressed because we do not like the feeling they generate inside us. When something bad or painful happens to us, we lock the feeling away to avoid the suffering the emotion causes. In extremely traumatic situations, such as severe physical or sexual abuse, the mind can sometimes hide or repress the memory of the event as a form of self-preservation. In these cases, people often feel uncomfortable in situations but do not know why. They are responding on a very subconscious level without a conscious attachment to the memory that is triggering the emotion.

For years, my default emotional response to almost any situation that made me feel uncomfortable was to get angry. Anger was an emotion I felt more comfortable processing. When something didn't go my way or someone would say something that made me upset, I would almost immediately get angry and lash out at that person. Not in a physical way, but in an emotional way. I'm not proud to say that for many years in my life, I was not the best person to be around or involved with. I was loving and kind but when I felt hurt, I would say mean things to people I loved. I felt anger toward them that I couldn't fully understand. It was how my mind processed the pain I felt. It took me years to uncover my pain and sadness and allow myself to feel it and process it in a healthy way before I could stop being so angry all the time.

That doesn't mean I don't get angry today. I do. I still have triggers that cause an emotional response that can be difficult to control within the moment. But I am now much more mindfully aware of the emotions as they rise up. I can quickly recognize that shift in my emotional state, and I can interrupt the pattern before I say or do something I will later regret.

So how do we accomplish this seemingly impossible task of controlling our thoughts so we can better direct our emotions? That is what this entire book is designed to do. Each chapter in this book has put you closer to developing the skills needed to do exactly that. Sometimes it is as simple as just being aware that something is happening. Changing our ability to look at a situation from a new perspective will shift your life in ways you can't even imagine. That is what happened to me. That is what continues to happen.

Learning to recognize what thoughts are generating emotions can be a challenge. Like everything discussed in this book, it is a skill that must be practiced and developed over time. Once you've recognized when these thoughts and emotions are appearing, you can apply what I like to call the alphabet approach to change your subconscious reaction to things that go on in your life.

This approach can be used in just about every situation, from dealing with another person to learning to deal with yourself. I call it the alphabet approach because there are 6 steps that make up the process – A, B, C, D, E, and F. Each one is a skill that we've worked on in previous chapters, which is why practice is so important. The more you master each step individually the easier it will be to put them all together when the moment arises.

These steps are as follows:

A – Awareness

The first step – like the first step in most aspects of this book

– is to become aware that you are experiencing a shift in your emotional state. For me, any time I feel a strong, overwhelming emotion inside, no matter if it's a positive or negative emotion, I practice becoming aware that a shift is taking place.

Most of us go through our day paying little attention to how we are feeling emotionally. We are on autopilot most of the time and never turn our attention inward. Hopefully, by the time you reach this point in the book, you've developed a practice of turning your attention inward on a more regular basis. This is important, because most of the things we are ever going to learn about ourselves begin with this same step. Being aware of how you feel, what you are thinking, and what you want to do points you in the right direction. Understanding our thoughts and emotions will always require us to first look at them and become aware of their existence. Because this is such a new experience, it naturally will lead into the second step.

B – Break the pattern

Because so much of our daily actions have become routine and expected, much of what we do has become a habit. This means the thinking, processing, and decision-making is more often than not happening on a subconscious level. By consciously becoming aware of what is going on, we add a new step in our normally habitual repetition. This extra step interrupts the flow and causes the mind to pause. The pattern and smoothness of the habit is thrown off, causing other parts of the mind to engage and assess what is going on. The brain realizes something is different, so it stops the flow of information and gives us time to pause and reassess what is happening.

This break in the habitual pattern of thinking is enough of a window for us to recognize the situation, giving us the opportunity to make a new choice, rather than simply following the same old pattern we've always followed. The neural pathway in the brain is interrupted just enough for us to consciously choose to go left when we normally, subconsciously, go right. This small change in process and pattern is enough to push your entire life in a new direction.

C – Calm Down

Once you've become aware of the pattern unfolding before you, and you've successfully interrupted the pattern of subconscious thought, take a moment for a few deep, calming breaths. Part of what keeps us going down the path of anger, frustration, sadness, fear, anxiety, or worry is that our body has already received direction from the mind and has begun its own protocol for the upcoming situation.

If you are fighting with someone, the mind has put you on the defensive and has signaled the body to prepare for war. Once this process begins, we must use our breathing to send new signals to the body that it is okay to relax and that war is not inevitable. Tension in the mind creates tension in the body. If we do not recognize the tension we feel in the body, our mind will still fight to keep us moving in the same direction because the tension is still present. Relaxing the body helps send the signal to the brain that you can turn off the adrenaline and that there are more options available than simply "fight, flight or freeze."

D – Describe the feelings

This part begins to allow your brain to switch from the emotional center to the rational one. Often when one part of the brain is more active, other parts become less active. When you go through the process of describing what it is you are feeling, it shifts your mind and engages the part of the brain that is responsible for focus and rational decisions. This area is known as the prefrontal cortex, and it is the part of our brain that is the newest, the most evolved, and what makes us different from all other beings that have brains.

The choices we make define who we are. Our personalities are comprised from the collection of choices we make, the actions we take, and the way we interact with the world around us. Some people are seen as having a positive, outgoing personality, while others are seen as being more disagreeable or abrasive. These characteristics are derived from how a person speaks and acts toward others. These choices are often a result of how well our prefrontal cortex functions. People who suffer damage to this part of the brain often report having changes in their personality. They begin to act differently because the part of the brain that controls our impulses, the manner in which we speak to people, and our ability to think about others has changed.

By going through the process of assigning descriptive words and phrases to what we are feeling, we force this part of our brain to engage, giving our emotional brain time to calm down and become less active.

E – Explore your thoughts

Now that your rational brain is more online and your emotional brain is a bit calmer, this is a good chance to begin to connect the dots between the thoughts you are having and the emotions rising inside you. This part of the process is reflective of the process we discussed back in the chapter about shadow work, or the process of healing old wounds. Often, our thoughts are connected with feelings based on previous interactions with people and situations that have forged our mental and emotional foundation. For many people, feelings of insecurity, worthlessness, lack of self-confidence, or painful experiences are kept hidden deep inside. The conscious mind may not be aware of these thoughts – but the subconscious mind is. When a situation, conversation, or a thought hits too close to these memories, the mind responds in different ways. We often get defensive and lash out as someone who has said something that makes us feel a way we do not like feeling.

Personally, I've always had issues with feeling as if I was of no value to others. If someone said something that made me feel as if what I had to say wasn't important, it would be a trigger for me to get angry and direct it toward the person. Many times, they had no idea they made me feel that way, nor did they understand my sudden emotional outburst. In truth, I didn't fully understand it, either. My anger seemed to rise from nowhere, and I could hardly control it.

By using this process of exploring my thoughts, I was able to find the connection between my thoughts and my emotions. I could then better realize that the reaction I was having was more about me than it was about what the person had said or done. This allowed me to move into the final step.

F – Forgive

This applies to both yourself and the person that is making you feel the way you feel. We often get upset with ourselves whenever we have an emotional outburst. We wish we could take back what we said, change the thoughts in our head, and have a do-over regarding the entire situation. This type of thinking leads to us feeling even worse, judging our actions and adding to the negative self-image we already struggle to improve.

Having emotions is not a bad thing. You should never get upset with yourself when you get emotional. It is a completely natural response to what's going on in your mind and in the world. You may not always handle emotional situations the way you want to, but you need to forgive yourself for how you acted or the things that you said.

And if someone said or did something that caused your emotional outburst, try to keep in mind that they, too, are dealing with their own thoughts and emotions. Their comments may come from a deep pain that they are unaware of. Finding compassion for another person and opening up our perspective about why they may act the way they do, say the things they do, or treat others the way they do will help you process your own thoughts and emotions. Learning to forgive others is a sign you understand that there is more going on behind the scenes than most of us are consciously aware of. Recognizing that truth about ourselves often helps us recognize that in others.

Practicing the art of forgiveness is key in learning to let go of the burden you carry in your heart, and it allows you to live a more loving and compassionate life.

* * *

A quiet sobbing came from the other room. It was loud enough to catch my ear, but not so loud as to be completely obvious that someone was trying to get my attention.

"Is that Lili?" I asked, already knowing the answer.

"Yes, she's up again," my wife, Deanna, responded.

I clumsily sat up and climbed out from underneath the warm blankets. The wood floor was cold and creaked beneath my feet as I made my way through the dark room, reaching for the door.

As I crossed the hallway and approached her room, I could already see her silhouette set against the harsh white light from her desk lamp, through her partially opened bedroom door. I knocked slightly, opened it, walked inside, and sat down at the foot of her bed. Her big, tear-filled eyes looked up at me and then quickly back down at her hands as they nervously fidgeted with the sheet.

"What's going on, Lili?"

"Are you mad at me?"

"No, honey, I'm not mad. I'm just trying to figure out what is going on."

"It's just that I can't do anything about anything. Nothing I do makes any difference."

I tried to piece together the events of the evening and what she might be referring to, with nothing coming to mind.

"I don't know what you are talking about. What do you mean, nothing you do makes any difference?"

She got very upset and started to breathe heavily and sob. I placed my hand on her shoulder and tried to calm her down.

"Okay. Just take a couple breaths with me."

I took a long, slow, and deliberate breath, encouraging her to mirror it. She did, and we continued to take two or three more deep, slow breaths together as she collected herself.

"It's just that," she continued, "I don't want anything to happen to you or Mom or anyone I love. But there's nothing I can do to stop that."

She started to sob again and then quickly took another breath so she could continue.

"Those people on the plane that hit the towers, they were just innocent people on a plane. There's nothing they could do."

I suddenly understood what was going on in her mind. The week before in one of her classes at school, they were talking about the events that took place on September 11, 2001, when planes hit the Twin Towers in New York. Ever since the class discussion, Lili had been having a hard time falling asleep. She kept thinking about what happened, about what the people on the planes and in the towers must have gone through. She struggled to make sense of the tragedy, much like the entire country did at the time. Honestly, I don't think there is a single person old enough to remember that hasn't lost at least one night of sleep thinking about that day.

"What if the same thing happened again? What if the plane crashed while we were on it? What if the plane crashes into our house while we are all asleep?"

Sadly, I recognized this pattern of thinking and worry. It was exactly what I suffered with growing up. The more I focused on the negative thoughts, the more they seemed to grow in intensity. No matter how farfetched the scenario in my mind may have appeared to anyone else, it seemed completely plausible and almost inevitable to me.

"I just don't want anything bad to happen to anyone I love," she repeated and began to sob again.

Again, I reminded her to breathe with me to try and calm her down.

"Honey, I know how you feel. What happened was very sad and

scary."

I wanted her to know that it was okay for her to be upset for the loss that had occurred. Recognizing and honoring our emotions is important. The last thing I wanted to do was to make her feel like there was something wrong with how she was feeling.

"And honey, right now, everyone you love is safe, happy, and okay. We are all tucked into our beds and sleeping comfortably with nothing like that to worry about. So what we need to do now is work on refocusing our mind away from the scary, negative stuff and on to something happier and more positive so you can sleep."

"Let's work on creating a new story to focus our attention on so we can stop focusing on the things that are making you sad and scared," I said, hoping she'd remember this process we'd used in the past when she would wake up from having a bad dream.

"Okay," she said as she began to lay her head down on her pillow. "I'll try."

"Perfect." I pulled the covers up and tucked her in.

"Let's think about a big, green field."

I began describing a large, grass-covered field that she could picture herself in. I told her to imagine what it felt like to have the grass tickle her feet as she walked through the open space. As she continued on, she could see a tree covered in big, green leaves. She could hear the sound of the leaves as the breeze blew, causing them to rattle and shake. Near the tree, there was a river running past. She could see the clear, blue water as it moved, bubbling past her and running over the rocks that sat on the edge of the river. Flowers bloomed on both sides of the river, their bright colors dancing across the rippling surface of the water.

I reminded her to focus on the very smallest of details and to study them with her mind. Try to look at every blade of grass, I told her, every leaf rustling on the tree, every petal connected to the flowers she could smell. If a negative thought started to slip back into her mind, I suggested she imagine the thought was just a picture on a large piece of paper. She could take that paper, crumple it up, drop it into the river and watch it slowly get swept away, out of sight.

Lili closed her eyes, and I kissed her forehead.

"Just keep your focus on the details of the field," I whispered as I slipped out the door, closing it just enough so I could barely see her through the opening.

I quietly slipped back into my room and returned to the warmth of my own blankets. As I closed my eyes, I thought about my daughter and her worry. I felt grateful that I was able to help her overcome her fear and fall back to sleep. I thought about that moment, so many years ago when I wondered how I would help my daughter if she worried. I had wondered how I would ever be able to help her if I could never help myself. I smiled, knowing I was able to teach her to calm her mind and focus her attention in the same way I had learned.

I became aware of a flood of images from the past ten years as they filled my mind. Quietly, I redirected my focus to the same field I had described to Lili. I could see all the details that she could see. I felt the grass and imagined placing my hand into the cool, crisp water. My mind became quiet and still.

I lay in bed, my heart filled with happiness knowing both Lili and I, in that moment, had learned to put aside our anxiety and rest peacefully.

That night we both fell asleep, together in the same field.

Free from our fear.

EPILOGUE: BRINGING IT ALL TOGETHER

As I sat in the church, hands sweaty and cold, I had the overwhelming feeling of being an adult for the very first time. I know that may sound strange coming from a man who is married with three children, but when you lose a parent, they take part of your childhood with them.

Hundreds of people packed the small, white church in Ashland, Massachusetts. Police officers lined the back two rows, dressed in full uniform. Most had worked with my father before he retired, while others were there simply out of respect for their fellow officers.

A few days earlier my brothers, sister, and I sat in the office of the funeral home discussing this very moment – our father's services. We all agreed, rather than one of us delivering a eulogy, each of us would take a moment and say a few words to remember our father. It seemed like the right decision at the time. But now, moments away from standing and speaking, I had my doubts.

    I took a quick glance down the pew. My wife and children sat, hands folded and eyes red. It all seemed surreal. The past 48 hours of services, handshakes, hugs, and condolences from so many people had me feeling overwhelmed, proud, inspired, and heartbroken, all at the same time. People, most of whom I had never met or even heard of, shared stories of how much my father had meant to them. Neighbors told me how he used to help plow their driveways, elderly people talked about how he always made time to stop and talk, and strangers shared how he had either bailed them out of trouble when they were younger or given them a chance when no one else would. Through each story and each encounter, I gained a new perspective of a man I realize now, I only partially knew. He meant something different to each person who came to pay their respects, each feeling the loss in their own unique way, and each remembering him through their own experiences and interactions. No two people knew him exactly the same way and no two people would mourn him the same way, either.

    When the time came for us to speak, all 5 of us, Patrick, Anthony, Laurie, Brendon, and I, walked to the front of the church. We decided to go by age, so Patrick spoke first. As he spoke, his voice cracked and his words trembled. I thought back to when we were kids. Doing whatever I could to make my big brother go first so I could see what would happen. He was always the bravest and he proved it again in that church.

    As he spoke, again I was struck with the uniqueness of his relationship to our father. Even though we were brothers and experienced all the same things, he remembered things I didn't and was impacted by moments that had slipped past me undetected.

    As he finished, I felt a lump rise in my throat. I wiped my eyes, stood and wrapped my arms around him. As if passing a very painful torch, he took my seat and I took his place behind the pulpit. With my words written on white, creased paper, laid out in front of me, I took a deep breath and looked out at the room. I felt a lot of things at that moment; loss, sadness, pain, a sense of wanting something back I would never have. My dad was gone and I would never see him again. I would never walk into a room and hear his big, gravely, "Hey, Stevie!" I'd never hug him, never hold his hand, laugh with him, or tell him I loved him again. All I could do now was stand up and say goodbye.

Here is what I said:

I inherited many traits from my father: his hairline, his inability to dunk a basketball or to reach things on the top shelf, his sarcastic sense of humor, his rugged good looks, his charm, and of course his humility. What I didn't inherit from him was his toughness. So I will do my best to get through this but I make no promises.

My father once told me that he never really liked speaking in front of people. That the first time he had to go and testify in court as a police officer he was terrified. Which surprised me because I didn't think he was afraid of anything. He said that the secret to getting over that fear was to be prepared. To go over your notes and know exactly what you wanted to say and if you did that, you'd be fine. But how do you prepare for this? To stand up here and saying goodbye to someone who meant so much to so many.

Growing up with my dad was not exactly what you would call a 'traditional' childhood. He taught me to fish, to catch a ball, to ride a bike, to be nice to people, and to look out for those who could not look out for themselves. He also taught me how to disarm an assailant, to break a chokehold, and to take someone down twice my size. When he took us to the movies, we didn't see ET, he took us to see Dirty Harry. And while other dads took their kids shopping at Toys R Us, he'd take Pat and me to the Army Navy Surplus Store.

My dad was a tough guy, through and through. And I wanted

to be just like him. He was my hero. He made me feel safe and protected. I always knew if I needed him, he would be there. In fact, my earliest memory of him was back when I was 3 years old. Patrick and I were up early and decided we were going to make breakfast. We jammed a bunch of bread into the toaster and went about dumping cereal into bowls and spilling milk around the kitchen, as kids tend to do. But the bread got stuck in the toaster and didn't pop. Eventually, the kitchen began filling up with smoke and all the fire alarms started going off. From around the corner, here comes my dad, in nothing but his tighty whities, running down the hall and into the kitchen to save us. That's how I'll always remember my dad. Always rushing in to help someone.

It's no wonder he was such a good police officer. I know he loved his family but I believe being a police officer was his first true love. Most dinners he would be sitting at the table, in his uniform with the cruiser running in the driveway. Eventually, his radio would crackle and he'd be out the door. He loved helping others. He loved wearing that badge. He was proud of the work he did and those he served with. I want to say thank you to all the brave men and women who wore that uniform with my dad, and to all those who continue to wear it today. You are all part of our family and dad loved you all very much.

But as tough as my dad was he also had a soft side—as much as he tried to hide it. All you had to do was see him with any of his grandchildren to know that. He loved being Nonno. And they loved him right back. I see a lot of my dad when I look at my children. Lili has his big heart. Noah is always on the move, just like my dad. And Camden, well I'm worried he may have gotten dad's devilish side… god, help us all!

I learned so much from him over the years. From the things he did well, and also from the things he didn't do so well. No one is perfect. But he always said if you make a mistake, you

have to own up and take responsibility. And I've always tried to do that. You tried to teach me how to be a good man but what you taught me in the process was how to be a great dad. Thank you for being such a great dad. I am so grateful I got to be your son. And I hope you were half as proud of me as I was of you.
I love you, dad. Rest easy. We'll take it from here.

When I sat down, I knew my life would never be the same – that I would never be the same. They say time heals all wounds. And in that moment, someplace deep inside, I knew it wouldn't always be this hard or hurt this much. The sadness I felt would slowly fade over time, but no matter how much it faded, it would never fully disappear. Instead, this experience, like all others, would become part of the journey. Moments like these become what makes us strong or makes us weak, what makes us determined or what discourages us, what makes us keep moving forward or what causes us to retreat. The quality of our life is not based simply on a collection of moments but on our ability to respond to those moments. This was a tough moment with the potential to either crush me or strengthen me. It all depended on how I responded and what I do moving forward.

In truth, I was now facing what my younger self always feared most – my father's death. It was something I never wanted to face but was inevitable. I've learned much about how to face my fears over the years – much of which I've written in this book – and that knowledge is what will get me through this now.

When I originally set out to write this book, my goal was simply to share my story and the things I've learned about navigating my own anxiety and fear. Learning to improve my relationship with myself became a gateway into my relationship with others. Seeing how I saw myself lifted the veil on how I saw the world around me. I began chipping away at the fear, and in the process, uncovered myself. Not the person I once was but the person I was becoming.

Anxiety had changed me – not for better or worse, just different.

Each lesson I learned and have shared had an impact on my life. Each impact shifted the trajectory of my future in the subtlest of way. But those subtle ways add up over time. Staying true to my course became about my ability to shift with each new discovery. Each moment presented to me became an opportunity – a challenge – I could rise up to meet it or fall beneath its weight. Some days I rose and some days I fell. But the sheer ability to recognize what each moment represented changed my life forever.

I no longer see myself as a victim of life and its circumstances. I see each moment as an opportunity to grow, to change, to evolve, and to experience the wonder that is this life we've been gifted. Often, I see this clearly. Other days, I do not. That is the nature of things. Life can often times get in the way of itself. We forget to be grateful and we feel rushed. We become overwhelmed with daily stress and we miss a chance to smile. We get so wrapped up in protecting the temporary state that we rob our self of the ability to marvel at its wonder and magic.

Some people live their entire life like this. Some of you have lived your entire life up until this point like that. My hope is, after reading this book you will become a little more aware of what is going on around you – and within you. You will learn to hear the voice and pause rather than blindly following its call. Having faith in yourself does not mean you have to believe everything you think. Our thoughts can be a source of great inspiration or a destructive force of nature. How we process these thoughts will dictate which they become. Only a mind that has learned to quiet itself and listen can know for sure which is which.

Your anxiety and fear have brought you here. They have been players in your life for many years and have shaped and molded the choices you've made and the life you've created. Do not reject this, but rather embrace it. Use this knowledge and experience your fear has given you to empower yourself to reclaim your creative abilities and direction. Use this negative force to your advantage.

You are not weak because you have suffered from anxiety. You are strong because you have faced this challenge head-on. It isn't about winning or losing – success or failure – it is about continuing to persist. It is about finding strength in the journey rather than always seeking the destination.

Your anxiety is part of your story but it isn't your entire story. Up until now, it has forced itself into a lead role. But you are the writer of this story. You are the director and you can take back control and recast your fear. You can change the role it plays in your life and make it a part of what makes you unique and special.

This book has armed you with the ideas, the insight, and the tools to take back your life and prioritize your fear in its proper place. Your goal should not simply to be comfortable. Being comfortable may feel nice at the time, but nothing grows there. No one ever changed the world by being comfortable and taking it easy. My hope is that you learn to prosper in the face of fear, for this truly renders fear powerless over you.

Fear is showing you the direction towards your greatness. It's leading you towards the life you've always wanted but never knew you could have. It is your minds attempt at shedding its old skin and metamorphosing into something else. What that is, depends on you and how far you are willing to go… and how far you are willing to grow?

I am so grateful for my anxiety. I am grateful for how bad things got and how much I hated my life. If my life had not become so bad, I would never have fought this hard to make it so amazing. My anxiety was the greatest gift I had ever received. It was the catalyst for all that has come into my life and all the things just beyond my grasp. If you find even the smallest nugget of help from this book, you can also be thankful for my anxiety, as well.

People love to ask what would you change about your life if you could go back and change something. Today, my honest answer is… nothing. I am who I am today because of what I've gone through. I don't know who I would be if I hadn't lived the life I've lived.

My hope for you is that you find this place in your life as well. The place where you can see each challenge in life as an opportunity to do something amazing. I hope that you learn to see your anxiety as a signal to take notice of what is going on, so that you may learn to process the feelings in a way that benefits your life rather than hinders it. Those butterflies each of us know so well can become a feeling you crave rather than one you avoid. Excitement and fear are opposite sides of the same coin. It is the element of the unknown that makes this so. Opening yourself to the idea of the unknown greatly increases what you are able to experience on this journey. And there is so much available to us in this life.

I hope this book helps you learn to love your life again. Because when we love life, amazing things can happen.

ACKNOWLEDGMENTS

I would like to take a moment and thank a few people that, without their love, support, and encouragement, this book would never have been possible.

To my wife, Deanna, thank you for always believing in me, supporting me, and loving me. You are my favorite. To my children, Lilianne, Noah, and Camden, you've all inspired me to be a better person. Never stop dreaming, growing, and learning. Dad loves you with all his heart! To my Mom, thank you for caring for me when I couldn't care for myself. Also, thanks for doing just enough damage so that I could write this book but not so much that I ended up in prison. To Louise, thank you for being a great Stepmom and for trying to make the best of a challenging situation. To my big brother, Patrick, thanks for leading the way, making me feel safe, and letting me tag along when we were kids. To Mike, Mark, Anthony, Laurie, Brendon, and Steven, I'm always here if you ever need anything! To Michael J. Chase, thank you for your guidance, your knowledge, and for sharing your story, your time, and your kindness with the world. To Pamme Boutselis, thank you for trusting that I could stand on a stage and share my story. I will forever be grateful. To my editor, Deidre Ashe, thank you for making it appear as if I have a decent grasp over the English language.

And, to my Dad, I'm sorry I didn't finish this book sooner. I miss you.

ABOUT THE AUTHOR

Steve Zanella is a husband, father, writer, speaker and creative professional. He has a passion for sharing his personal journey overcoming anxiety and depression with those who stand to benefit most. Through meditation, mindfulness and learning to live in the present moment, he has refocused his life on helping others.

If you would like to learn more, please visit: www.stevezanella.com

"We are all just walking each other home."

~ Ram Dass

www.ingramcontent.com/pod-product-compliance
Lightning Source LLC
LaVergne TN
LVHW051550070426
835507LV00021B/2509